D1306001

ACCOUNTING

HISTORY AND THOUGHT

EDITED BY
RICHARD P. BRIEF
New York University

A GARLAND SERIES

THE STORY OF THE FIRM
1864-1964
Clarkson, Gordon & Co.

GARLAND PUBLISHING, INC.

New York & London

1989

Library of Congress Cataloging-in-Publication Data

The Story of the firm 1864–1964, Clarkson, Gordon & Co.
p. cm. — (Accounting history and thought)
Reprint. Originally published: Toronto : Clarkson, Gordon & Co., 1964.
ISBN 0-8240-3610-7 (alk. paper)
1. Clarkson, Gordon & Co.—History. 2. Accounting firms—Canada—History.
I. Clarkson, Gordon & Co. II. Series.
HF5616.C23C537 1989
338.7'61657'0971—dc20   89-23275

Printed on acid-free 250-year-life paper

Manufactured in the United States of America

THE
STORY OF THE FIRM
1864-1964

Clarkson, Gordon & Co.

THOMAS CLARKSON

THE
STORY OF THE FIRM
1864 – 1964

Clarkson, Gordon & Co.

FOREWORD

As the firm approached its 100th birthday the partners of Clarkson, Gordon & Co. recognized the need to record the history of the firm and we asked one of our number, Mr. A. J. Little, to undertake this task. Many others, partners and friends, have helped in gathering data and recalling memories of former days. But most of the research, the selection of the material, and the writing of the story fell to him. It was for him a labour of love, but we know that it also proved to be both time consuming and demanding. We are all very grateful for the effort and the result.

In planning this book two basic decisions were made. First, it should not be a history of a firm in the sense of being an analysis and interpretation of the interplay of the economic and social forces and of the personalities which, taken together, account for the transformation of the small local firm of 1864 into the large national firm of today. To make such a historical study would require a calm detachment which none of us, whose professional lives have been spent wholly within the firm, could possibly bring to the task. Secondly, it should not deal with the contributions which present partners, managers and staff have made and are making to the firm's development. These, we have concluded, may more safely be left to a later volume of the Clarkson, Gordon story.

Our 100th birthday is only one point in time in a continuing and unfolding record. But though it is a point in time, a 100th birthday none the less is an important date for a firm, just as it is for a person. It is a time for pride, and a time of challenge.

A 100th birthday is a time for pride—and the present partners, managers and staff are proud indeed of the inheritance we have received. In these pages will be found the story of our founders—Thomas, E. R. C., and G. T. Clarkson, Colonel Gordon (fortunately still with us), and R. J. Dilworth. These men were giants in the profession in their time and they laid well the foundations on which others have built. The present partners recognize the trust which has been imposed upon them by these founders and the need for never ending vigilance to ensure that the standards they established are maintained and passed on untarnished to future generations.

The founding partners did not labour alone, however, and being modest men they would be sorry that no reference or only slight reference has been made to many former partners, managers, and staff who worked with them to build the firm of today. Necessarily the history of a firm must pick and choose a few individuals and highlights out of a multitude of persons and events, and the sheer numbers of those who have been with us over the years makes it an impossibility to record their individual contributions. You will find their names in the Appendixes of this book. When you note how many graduates of the firm hold highly responsible positions in Canadian business, government, academic, and professional circles you will understand why our sense of pride encompasses them. Not only are we proud of their achievements since they left us—we are grateful for the contribution they made to the firm when they were with us.

Most of all, a 100th birthday is a time of challenge. Our predecessors met many challenges in their time. Only because they did so was it possible to develop the practice of one man living in Toronto into a national firm with 79 partners carrying on a practice in 12 cities across Canada and in two languages. We and our successors must be equally alert to the challenges of the future. We will have to adapt our skills, and where necessary learn new skills, to meet the changing needs of our clients and to ensure a satisfying professional life for the partners, managers, and staff which comprise the firm. Only if we do so can we be worthy of the first hundred years of the Clarkson, Gordon story.

J. R. M. WILSON

ACKNOWLEDGEMENT

It is fortunate that over the years the firm has saved bits and pieces of important information that have made this historical sketch possible. Most important of all is a set of notes which Colonel Gordon prepared some years ago as a background for a firm history, and in which he in turn had incorporated information recorded by other early partners. Much of the very early background was obtained from documents retained by various members of the Clarkson family, and through discussions with them.

There is a wealth of fascinating information about early Toronto available in the reference libraries of the city, and most useful of all were the volumes of Robertson's *Landmarks of Toronto*. We are indebted to the Toronto *Telegram* for permission to produce two illustrations (Figs. 5 and 6) from cuts contained in those volumes, and to Professor Eric Arthur for two drawings (Figs. 9 and 10) which appear also in *Toronto: No Mean City* (University of Toronto Press, 1964). A debt of gratitude is also owed to Miss Jean Houston of the editorial staff of the University of Toronto Press for her helpful and constructive criticism of the text as it was being prepared.

In order to allow for adequate printing time, it was necessary to close the lists of staff as of July 1, 1964. We all regret that it was not possible to include the names of those joining the firm subsequent to that date.

July 1964   A.J.L.

CONTENTS

ILLUSTRATIONS

IMPORTANT DATES

IN THE HISTORY OF THE FIRM

1832 Thomas Clarkson came to York, Upper Canada

1864 Thomas Clarkson appointed an official Assignee by the Province of Canada

1870 E. R. C. Clarkson joined his father's firm

1872 Thomas Clarkson retired, E. R. C. Clarkson formed the partnership of Clarkson and Munro (dissolved 1877)

1874 Thomas Clarkson died

1877 E. R. C. Clarkson appointed an official Assignee and formed the firm Turner, Clarkson & Co. (dissolved 1881)

1881 E. R. C. Clarkson commenced practice in his own name

1891 E. R. C. Clarkson and W. H. Cross formed an accounting partnership, Clarkson & Cross

1893 G. T. Clarkson joined his father's firm

1896 F. C. Clarkson joined his father's firm

1898 H. D. L. Gordon joined Clarkson & Cross

1905 H. D. L. Gordon established his own practice

1906 E. G. Clarkson joined his father's firm

1907 H. D. L. Gordon and R. J. Dilworth formed the partnership of Gordon & Dilworth

1913 Clarkson & Cross and Gordon & Dilworth merged to form the firm of Clarkson, Gordon & Dilworth, Chartered Accountants (Mr. W. H. Cross retired)

E. R. C. Clarkson & Sons formed to continue the trustee practice

Both firms moved to 15 Wellington Street West

1922 Montreal office opened

1928 The firm of Clarkson, McDonald, Currie & Co. formed in Montreal (dissolved in 1935) and in Toronto the firm name became Clarkson, Gordon, Dilworth, Guilfoyle & Nash

1929 An office opened in Windsor (closed 1934) and in Ottawa (closed 1937)

1931 E. R. C. Clarkson died

1935 H. E. Guilfoyle died, and firm name became Clarkson, Gordon, Dilworth & Nash

1938 Hamilton office opened

1939 The firm became associated with The J. D. Woods Co. Limited, which later became Woods, Gordon & Co.

1943 R. J. Dilworth died

1944 A. E. Nash died

The partnership of Arthur Young, Clarkson, Gordon & Co. was formed

1945 Vancouver office opened

1946 Names changed to Clarkson, Gordon & Co., and The Clarkson Company

1948 London office opened

Merger with Black, Hanson & Co. in Winnipeg

Vancouver practice merged with that of Harold D. Campbell

1949 G. T. Clarkson died

Merger with Richardson & Graves in Calgary

1952 Merger with Read, Smith & Forbes in Regina

1954 The Clarkson Company partnership was dissolved and The Clarkson Company Limited was incorporated

1955 London practice merged with that of Charles T. Sears

1956 Merger with Kinnaird, Aylen & Co. in Edmonton

Calgary practice merged with that of William Macintosh

1957   Merger with K. Douglas MacLennan in Windsor

1959   Vancouver practice merged with that of Carter, Reid & Walden

A partnership was formed in Brazil with the name Arthur Young, Clarkson, Gordon & Co., with offices in Rio de Janeiro and Sao Paulo

1960   Calgary practice merged with Harvey, Morrison & Co.

1962   Merger with Davis, Dunn & Broughton in Kitchener and London, and with Scully & Scully in Kitchener

Quebec office opened and merger with DeCoster, Normandeau & Cie.

THE
STORY OF THE FIRM
1864 - 1964

Clarkson, Gordon & Co.

Chapter I

MR. THOMAS CLARKSON

Thomas Clarkson was born in Sussworth in the County of Lincolnshire, England, on January 26, 1802, and in 1832 came to the town of York, Upper Canada. York was a small town with a population of about eight thousand, and was not incorporated as a city until 1834 at which time its name was changed to Toronto. Upper Canada was still a separate colonial province of British North America. The Act of Union, 1841, created the united Province of Canada, and that part formerly known as Upper Canada came to be known as Canada West, although that name apparently had no legal status.

Mr. Clarkson had been married in England but his first wife died in 1829 before he came to

Canada. He married again in Canada in 1834, but his second wife also died very early in life, and in 1844 he married for a third time. Mr. Clarkson had two children in England through his first marriage, four through his second marriage, and ten through his third, or sixteen children in all. His third wife was Sarah Helliwell, daughter of a prominent Toronto family of that day, and they were married in St. James' Cathedral on May 2, 1844. Their fifth child, Edward Roper Curzon, was the son who would later carry on the family business.

In the early days Thomas Clarkson was a retail merchant; later he operated an auctioneering business, and about 1850 established a produce and commission business on Front Street, apparently specializing in the grain trade. Records of his activity from 1832 to 1860 are incomplete, and the earliest official document found which refers to Thomas Clarkson is the Toronto Commercial Directory for 1836-37 which lists him as a storekeeper at 55 Yonge Street. This is confirmed by information contained in *The Windmill*, a story of the early days of Messrs. Gooderham and Worts. In a listing of their principal customers in 1838 there appears: "Thomas Clarkson & Co., general storekeeper, 55 Yonge Street, on ground now occupied by the R. Simpson Co." Later in that same history, in dealing with business conditions and sales volume for 1840, there is the following reference to the store:

"Best" whiskey brought 2s. 6d. by the barrel and was in better demand—the sales amounting to nearly 1300 gallons, of which Thomas Clarkson & Co. took nearly 850. It will be remembered that this shop was at the Yonge Street corner of Macaulay Town and the demand for a better quality here possibly indicated an improvement in the residential character of the western and northern districts.

In the eighteen-thirties "Macaulay Town" was the name given to the property on the north side of Queen Street (then called Lot Street) from Yonge Street to Osgoode Hall.

Reference to the corner of Yonge Street and Macaulay Town clearly indicates the southwest corner of Yonge and Queen streets. This means that the Thomas Clarkson store must have occupied the site which, in 1869, became the first location of the T. Eaton Company, and later became the site of the Robert Simpson Company.

The store on Yonge Street was probably operated until about 1842. Thomas Clarkson was still listed as a merchant in the City of Toronto Poll Book for 1841, but the Toronto Directory and Street Guide for 1843-44 (the next directory listing that could be found) shows Thos. Clarkson & Co. as auctioneers at the corner of King and New Streets (New Street ran north and south between King and Queen streets, later became Nelson Street and is now a part of Jarvis Street). He operated this business for some seven or eight years and then opened a produce and commission business on Front Street.

From 1850 until he moved to the United States in 1860, Thomas Clarkson was a prominent member of the Toronto business community. His business prospered and he found time to take an active part in other business and community affairs. He was President of the Commercial Building & Investment Society which was incorporated in 1851 and became one of the important building societies of the day. It was patterned after the English building societies which were formed to finance housing construction. Thomas Clarkson was also one of the promoters of the Toronto and Georgian Bay Canal Company. In 1852 he became the second President of the Toronto Board of Trade, of which he was one of the incorporators. In a tribute written in 1937 the then President, Mr. J. J. Gibbons, said:

On February 10th, 1845, The Toronto Board of Trade was incorporated by Act of Parliament, and the name of Thomas Clarkson appears among the list of incorporators. In 1852, Mr. Clarkson became the second president of the Board, and continued in that office for six years. It was during the presidency of

Thomas Clarkson that the Board advocated the repeal of the usury laws, changes in postal regulations by which British mails were forwarded direct from Atlantic steamships to Toronto, the erection of a new and adequate Post Office in the city, the increase of commercial facilities by means of railway lines from Toronto (including the daily operation of a steam railway from Toronto to Newmarket), and many other matters of vital importance to the growing city. And it is interesting to note that these proposals, so advanced and advocated by the Board of Trade, all materialized before Thomas Clarkson resigned the presidency in 1858.

The new Post Office referred to by Mr. Gibbons was built in 1853 at No. 10 Toronto Street, and is now the head office of Argus Corporation.

In 1856 Mr. Clarkson took part in the development of the Bank of Toronto. The history of the Toronto-Dominion Bank, *100 Years of Banking in Canada,* says (p. 8): "Meanwhile successful efforts had been made to acquire technical and financial wisdom for the higher echelons. Thomas Clarkson, who was then President of the Commercial Building and Investment Society and a prominent Toronto financier, appeared at the first formal meeting of the board of directors on July 1, 1856."

The first advertisement of the Bank appears on page 7. It is interesting to note from this advertisement that as late as 1856 the official currency in Canada was sterling. In 1858 the Currency Act was passed and at that time the decimal system now in use became the official unit of account for Canada.

Mr. Clarkson also took an active interest in civic and cultural affairs. His name crops up in various events which took place in St. Lawrence Hall as recorded in the third volume of Robertson's *Landmarks of Toronto*. For example, in June 1858, a very large audience enjoyed a presentation of Handel's oratorio of Judas Maccabaeus in the Hall, and Thomas Clarkson, President of the Board of Trade, was

BANK OF TORONTO
(Chartered by Act of Parliament)
Capital......£500,000
In 20,000 shares of £25 each
OFFICE—CHURCH ST. (Late CITY BANK)

Directors

James G. Chewett Esq.—President
William Gamble, Esq.—Vice-President

Thomas Clarkson, Esq. Geo. Michie, Esq.
John Brunskill, Esq. James Crawford, Esq.

Henry John Boulton, Esq.

ANGUS CAMERON, ESQ.—CASHIER
The Bank is now open for the transaction of
general business.

Interest will be allowed at the rate of three
per cent on current accounts and at the rate
of four per cent on permanent deposits.

By order of the Board

Angus Cameron
Cashier

Toronto, July 17, 1856.

listed as one of the distinguished patrons, which included
such notables as Sir John Beverley Robinson and John A.
Macdonald. On an earlier occasion he was a speaker, along
with George Brown, M.P.P., at a public festival in the Hall
in connection with the Early Closing Association, under the
patronage of the merchants of Toronto. Later on he became
one of the early members of the York Pioneers, a society
formed by citizens who had resided in the Town of York.
This is a historical society which is now known as the
York Pioneer and Historical Society.

In 1860 he left Toronto and moved to Milwaukee, Wis-
consin, where he formed a grain brokerage business with
his sons Benjamin Reid Clarkson and Robert Guy Clarkson

under the name of Thomas Clarkson & Sons. The Toronto business was continued by the partnership of Clarkson Hunter & Co.

Chapter 2

THOMAS CLARKSON & CO.
1864-1872

Thomas Clarkson returned to Toronto in 1864,
and this is the date of the real beginning of the
present business. In that year he was appointed
an Official Assignee by the Province of Canada
and commenced developing his trustee and
receivership business. This form of business subsequently led, as it did for other firms, to the
establishment of an independent accounting practice. There were, of course, no chartered accountants in Canada in those early days. The earliest
formal Accounting Society was formed in Edinburgh in 1854 but the Ontario Institute was not
incorporated until 1883. Mr. Clarkson also re-
established in 1864 his earlier business as commission agent and wholesale dealer in grain and

stocks, and acted as an insurance agent; all his businesses were transacted from premises at 83 Front Street East.

By the time that Mr. Clarkson established the trustee business in 1864, Toronto had become a thriving financial centre, An engraving of the city as it appeared in 1864 is shown as Plate 1. It had grown in population to 48,000, about six times the size it was when he first arrived in 1832. The city was well served with banks, including

THE BANK OF MONTREAL   THE BANK OF UPPER CANADA
THE BANK OF TORONTO   THE CITY BANK
THE ONTARIO BANK   THE QUEBEC BANK
THE COMMERCIAL BANK OF CANADA
(at 15 Wellington Street West)
THE BANK OF BRITISH NORTH AMERICA

It is interesting to note that only two of those eight banks exist in 1964; the others failed or were absorbed by other banks. There were other important banks in British North America in 1864, such as the Bank of Nova Scotia (founded 1832), but, because of distance and difficulty of communication, these did not operate throughout the country.

The city was then being served by a public transportation system provided by the Toronto Street Railway Company, which was formed in 1861 and enjoyed a franchise to operate horse-drawn vehicles in the city. According to its history, in December of 1861 it had 11 cars, 70 horses, a number of sleighs and wagons, and 6 miles of track. The city streets and many houses and places of business were lighted with gas, supplied by the Consumer's Gas Company, incorporated in 1848. Transportation to and from the city was also good, and the Grand Trunk, the Great Western, and the Northern Railways all ran into the first Union station at the foot of York Street.

The year 1864 was a historic one for Canada. For some time the maritime provinces had been considering a confederation and were planning a conference to discuss the

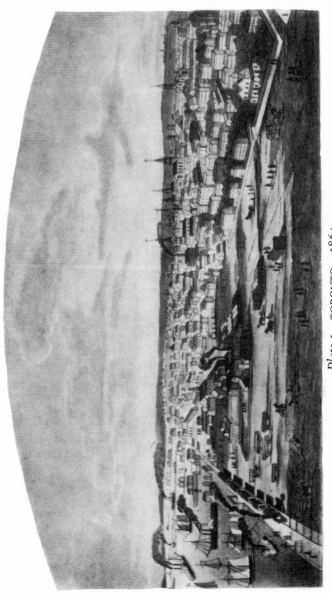

Plate I TORONTO—1864

Plate 2 THE CLARKSON ELEVATOR — 1869

matter. The far-sighted John A. Macdonald was thinking along similar lines for the whole of British North America, and persuaded the governments of the maritime provinces to invite representatives of the Province of Canada to attend. The conference was held in Charlottetown in September 1864. This led to certain general areas of agreement, and was followed by the Quebec Conference in October of 1864. From that point three of the four provinces (Prince Edward Island remaining aloof) moved slowly but steadily towards the Confederation of 1867, at which time the Province of Canada was divided into the two provinces Ontario and Quebec, which, with Nova Scotia and New Brunswick, formed the Dominion of Canada.

Business conditions had not been good in Canada for two or three years. Trade with the United States was seriously disrupted by the American Civil War, which in 1864 had been in progress about three years and was to continue through most of 1865 (President Lincoln was shot April 14, 1865). Crops had been poor, and *The Story of the Canada Permanent Mortgage Corporation 1855-1925* records: "In 1864 for the third successive year, there was a deficient harvest, due in a great measure to an extraordinary drought and to the ravages of the midge." In spite of these conditions, or perhaps because of them, Mr. Clarkson's businesses flourished, particularly the trustee business.

In 1869 he expanded in a new direction by acquiring through a bankruptcy a grain storage elevator on the waterfront. This was promptly renamed "Clarkson's Elevator" and a sketch of it is shown in Plate 2. The engraved announcement card which Mr. Clarkson sent to his customers is reproduced as Figure 1.

Toronto, July 31st, 1869.

DEAR SIR,

We take pleasure in notifying you that we have become proprietors of **MESSRS. BEARD & SONS' ELEVATOR,** *and in connection with our* **Commission Business** *we are prepared to do a* **General Storage and Forwarding Business.**

The arrangement and Capacity of the Elevator, together with its close proximity to our Market, will enable us to offer excellent facilities for selecting Grain, without fear of admixture.

Any orders for the purchase of Grain, &c., entrusted to us shall meet with prompt and careful attention.

Liberal arrangements made for buying, storing, and shipping grain.

Soliciting your patronage, we remain,

Your most obedient servants,

THOMAS CLARKSON & CO.

Elevator—Foot of East Market Street.

Figure 1 THE 1869 ANNOUNCEMENT

Mr. Clarkson was extremely pleased with the new acquisition, and in writing about it in August 1869 to his son Edward Roper Curzon Clarkson, who was then working in Montreal, he said: "This is Beards' Elevator we have taken for five years. We have half the net proceeds for working it. I consider this one of the best bargains I ever made—the prospects are that we shall have as much as we can do." This turned out to be the case, and before long he was urging E.R.C. to return to take over a part of the trustee business. Mr. Thomas Munro, his senior employee, was spending full time on that business and Mr. Clarkson found that he was turning down new work because of lack of experienced help. Furthermore, he was getting on in years (he was then 67) and was finding the business strenuous. He wrote to E.R.C. in September: "I have now a Bankrupt Estate at Penetanguishene—have been there once, rode 80 miles in a stage coach or spring waggon, which was too much fatigue for me."

Apparently E. R. C. Clarkson was under contract of some sort and was not free to return immediately in spite of urging by his father. However, he did return to Toronto to join his father's firm early in 1870. Mr. Thomas Clarkson was forced to retire from business because of ill health in 1872, and the trustee and bankruptcy business was carried on by Mr. Munro and E.R.C.

Mr. Clarkson's commission business and grain trade was carried on for a few years by his son Benjamin Reid Clarkson, one of the two sons who had carried on a similar business in Milwaukee. Benjamin formed a new firm, Clarkson, Hagarty & Grassett, a few years later, but this firm was dissolved on July 15, 1876, and this apparently terminated the Clarkson participation in that business.

Mr. Thomas Clarkson died in Toronto on May 4, 1874, and was buried in St. James' Cemetery.

Chapter 3

THE CLARKSON FIRMS
1872-1913

E. R. C. Clarkson (see Plate 3) was born on August 11, 1852, at 278 King Street East, Toronto, the home of his father, Thomas Clarkson. In September of 1864 he commenced his studies at Upper Canada College which had been opened in Toronto some thirty-four years earlier at the corner of King and Simcoe streets. He graduated in June of 1867 and was sent by his father to Montreal to gain mercantile experience. Lewis, Kay & Co., a wholesale drygoods firm, employed him at £25 per annum. In 1870, at the age of seventeen, he returned to Toronto and joined the family business.

E.R.C. devoted his full time to the trustee work, and by the time his father was compelled

Plate 3   **E. R. C. CLARKSON**

Plate 4   W. H. CROSS

to retire in 1872 because of poor health, he was fully conversant with that business and quite ready to take over. Unfortunately, he was still under twenty-one and was not eligible to receive the appointment as official assignee of the Government..Accordingly, the appointment went to his employee, Mr. Munro, and a new partnership was formed, Clarkson and Munro, which continued the business from 1872 until 1877. In that year Mr. E. R. C. Clarkson was appointed an official assignee and he joined a Mr. Turner in the firm of Turner, Clarkson & Co. That firm continued until 1881 when E.R.C. commenced to practise under his own name alone.

About this time he was becoming very interested in the practice of accountancy, and was one of twelve sponsors who called a special meeting of accountants in 1879 to discuss the organization of an accounting society. This resulted in the formation of the Institute of Accountants and Adjusters of Canada in December of 1879, and E. R. C. Clarkson was elected as one of nine members of the first council. In 1883 he was one of the petitioners for the charter of the Institute of Chartered Accountants of Ontario and soon thereafter presented himself for the examinations so that he would be entitled to use the designation "Chartered Accountant." He later became a President of the Institute. He conducted an accounting practice in his own name until 1891 and then formed the partnership of Clarkson & Cross, which also handled the trustee and bankruptcy work.

Mr. W. H. Cross (Plate 4) was born in Manchester May 15, 1845, and was trained as an accountant in England before coming to Canada. He went first to Hamilton and later moved to Toronto. In 1890 Mr. Clarkson engaged him to assist in the accounting practice and formed a partnership with him the following year. Like Mr. Clarkson he was one of the founders of the Ontario Institute. Mr. Cross was apparently a brilliant man and a wizard with figures.

The financial record of the accounting practice for 1890 was as follows:

Fees earned		$6,947
Unpaid	$2,800	
Uncharged	480	
		3,280
		$3,667
Expenses		1,674
		$1,993
Drawn by W. H. Cross		2,115
Advanced by E. R. C. Clarkson		$ 122

Mr. E. R. C. Clarkson, like his father, had a very large family, seven sons and five daughters. Three of his sons joined him in the business. Geoffrey Teignmouth joined the firm in 1893 at the age of fifteen, Frederick Curzon in 1896 at the age of sixteen, and Edward Guy in 1906 at the age of eighteen. Of the three, only Mr. G.T. sat for the accountancy examinations, and he was active in both the trustee work and in the accounting practice. Plate 5 is a picture of the three brothers taken at a dinner held in 1946 in honour of Mr. G. T. Clarkson and Colonel Gordon.

In this early period one of the accounting students in the firm was John F. Helliwell, a relative of Mr. E. R. C. Clarkson (whose mother was Sarah Helliwell), who was articled to Mr. Cross. In 1897 John Helliwell went to Vancouver to establish the firm of Clarkson, Cross & Helliwell which continued until 1910. However, because it was so remote from Toronto and communication facilities were not good, neither firm contributed much to the other and by mutual agreement the association was terminated. Mr. John F. Helliwell continued in practice in Vancouver and the well-known firm he founded is now Helliwell, Maclachan & Co.

Plate 5 E. G. CLARKSON, F. C. CLARKSON, AND G. T. CLARKSON

A similar arrangement was made with John H. Menzies who opened the Winnipeg firm of Clarkson, Cross and Menzies in 1903, which continued until 1913. John Menzies was an Englishman who trained in London and worked in China before coming to Canada. He was a senior member of the staff of Clarkson & Cross in Toronto before going to Winnipeg. A part of the announcement sent to clients and placed in the newspapers at the time is reproduced as Figure 2. This was a large folded document, and on the

(CANADA)

CLARKSON & CROSS

CHARTERED ACCOUNTANTS

TRUSTEES, RECEIVERS, LIQUIDATORS

E. R. O. CLARKSON, F.O.A.
W. H. CROSS, F.O.A.

ONTARIO BANK CHAMBERS,
33 SCOTT STREET,
TORONTO.

CLARKSON, CROSS & HELLIWELL

MOLSON'S BANK CHAMBERS,

VANCOUVER,
(AND AT VICTORIA)

POWERS OF ATTORNEY TO BE ISSUED TO
JOHN F. HELLIWELL, F.O.A.(CAN.)

BRITISH COLUMBIA.

CLARKSON, CROSS & MENZIES

MOLSON'S BANK BUILDING,

228 PORTAGE AVENUE,

WINNIPEG,

POWERS OF ATTORNEY TO BE ISSUED TO
JOHN H. MENZIES.

MANITOBA.

ESTABLISHED 1864.

E. R. C. CLARKSON

COMMISSIONER FOR ADMINISTERING OATHS TO BE USED IN MANITOBA AND ONTARIO.

A.B.C. CABLE AND TELEGRAPH CODES.

Figure 2 THE 1903 ANNOUNCEMENT

inside was the announcement of opening the Winnipeg office which said in part:

"Prompt and efficient attention will be given to the special examination or the periodical audit of the company or other accounts, and of branches or agencies in the North West; to financial commissions in Ontario, Quebec, and England, and to the administration and care of property or of any business interest committed to our charge."

Mr. E. R. C. Clarkson had a fine reputation in the business community, and his advice and counsel were particularly sought by the banks. He was able to wind up businesses quickly and realize cash for the creditors. However, he did not think this policy was good for Canada or the banks or, in fact, for any of the large creditors. Finally, he persuaded one of the banks to let him manage one of the companies which was in difficulty instead of winding it up. He was able to pull the company out of its difficulties and this was very important to the small community where it was located, as well as continuing a profitable client for the bank.

In 1912 Mr. E.R.C. was elected a director of the Canada Permanent Mortgage Corporation and in 1922 was elected a Vice-President. In 1914 he was elected a director of the Manufacturers Life Insurance Company, and held these and other important posts until his death in 1931.

A young accountant employed by the Clarkson & Cross firm in 1898 was Harry Duncan Lockhart Gordon, about whom more will be learned in the next chapter.

Chapter 4

GORDON & DILWORTH
1907-1913

A most significant date in the history of the development of the present firm is 1907, the year that H. D. L. Gordon and R. J. Dilworth formed a partnership to practise accounting under the name Gordon & Dilworth.

H. D. L. Gordon was born in Toronto on July 20, 1873, on Windsor Street, a little street running north and south between Wellington and Front streets just west of John Street. His father had emigrated to Canada from Scotland in 1868 and practised law in Toronto. H. D. L. Gordon, the eldest of nine children, attended Upper Canada College, and went on to the Royal Military College at Kingston, graduating in 1894. After graduation he worked for a short time as bookkeeper for an exchange broker who dealt in sterling exchange for the banks. As there seemed little prospect for advancement he decided to study for his c.a. degree and after consulting with Mr. E. R. C. Clarkson, went to England for two and one-half years where he was employed by Messrs. Cooper Brothers & Co., a large firm of accountants in London. They granted him all the privileges of an articled clerk without requiring payment of the usual premiums, but of course paid him no salary. In 1898 he passed the final examination of the Society of Incorporated Accountants and Auditors (an English society since merged with the Institute of Chartered Accountants in England and Wales) and returned to Canada. That same year he was granted the degree of Chartered Accountant by the Ontario Institute.

In 1898 Mr. Gordon joined the staff of Clarkson & Cross in Toronto and was employed by that firm for about eight years. In 1905 he planned to get married, and as the firm had no partnership opportunity available for him, they mutually agreed he might do better on his own. He then left Clarkson & Cross, married on February 22, 1905, and opened his own accounting practice. His first assignment was to manage the Penny Bank, which provided him with office space, a stenographer, and a small honorarium. Many of the present and former staff members will remember the Penny Bank which provided a system through which school children could save their pennies and deposit them at their schools. It was incorporated in 1905, and H. D. L. Gordon was its first Manager, and retained this post until 1913. The Penny Bank stopped taking deposits during the Second World War (when the Government was selling War Savings Certificates to school children) and shortly thereafter was wound up and taken over by the Post Office Savings Bank.

Mr. Gordon's business grew quickly so that in less than a year it was necessary to find a competent assistant. In

1906 he engaged a graduate accountant by the name of R. J. Dilworth.

Robert James Dilworth was born in Trinity Square, Toronto, on February 13, 1869, son of James Dilworth of Belfast, Ireland, who had come to Canada as a soldier. After graduation from Dufferin Public School and Jarvis Collegiate, R.J. worked for various employers as office boy, bookkeeper, and office manager, including at one point Mr. G. T. Clarkson. A general letter of reference written by G. T. Clarkson, on August 12, 1901, said: "Mr. R. J. Dilworth was in the employ of the Consolidated Pulp & Paper Co. Ltd., Toronto,—upon its going into liquidation we found his books well kept, accurate and in good order— He has since and up to date been employed by us in such liquidation and has given entire satisfaction, proving to be capable and with ability." Perhaps because of his experience with the Clarkson firm, R. J. Dilworth decided to obtain his accounting degree, and, at the age of thirty-two, articled to Messrs. Jenkins & Hardy, where he obtained his c.a. degree in 1903.

H. D. L. Gordon approached R. J. Dilworth and offered him a position at an annual salary, with R.J. to have the right to develop business for his own account provided it took no more than half his time. The letter of understanding written by H. D. L. Gordon on March 3, 1906, is reproduced as Figure 3. The arrangement between them proved satisfactory and profitable from the start and one year later, on April 1, 1907, they formed the partnership known as Gordon & Dilworth. Under the first partnership agreement H. D. L. Gordon had a two-thirds interest in the profit, with Mr. Dilworth having one-third. Volume continued to grow with R.J. obtaining an increasing share of new work, so that as of April 1, 1911, they signed a new agreement under which profits were shared equally.

A clear indication of the growth and prosperity of the new firm is given by its financial statements. For the year

H. D. LOCKHART GORDON, A.S.A.A., F.C.A. (can.)

Chartered Accountant

REPRESENTED · QUEBEC
MONTREAL

CORNER YORK AND RICHMOND STREETS
TELEPHONE M. 4973

TORONTO,_____**Mar.** 3/06._____190__

R. J. Dilworth, Esq.,

     Toronto.

Dear Sir:-

     In pursuance of our conversation yesterday I am prepared to make the following offer, to engage you as my assistant for one year from the First day of April, 1906, at a salary of $1500.00 per annum, payable by monthly instalments. This engagement to be terminated by either party on three months' notice in writing. You to have the privilege of doing business on your own account as a Chartered Accountant on the understanding that half of any fees you may charge for wrok done for your own clients should be applied in the reduction of the salary I am to pay you, and you to have the privilege of undertaking as much work of this sort as you can get, as long as the work does not take up more than half your time.

     If at the end of the year we do not care to make any fresh arrangements it to be distinctly understood that any clients we have obtained are to be considered as our own, and that we are each to refuse to take any work from any of each others clients. This offer to remain open from one week from date and the understanding being that if you accept the same you will be able to begin work for me on the First day of April ,1906.

        Yours faithfully.

Figure 3 THE 1906 LETTER

ended March 31, 1907, Mr. Dilworth had enjoyed a salary of $1,500 and a share of profits of about $1,000—Mr. Gordon's income was a little larger. For the ten months ended January 31, 1913, the last period of operation of the partnership, the statement was as follows:

Net fees		$36,314.02
Expenses	$12,640.27	
Bad debts	451.60	
Commissions	340.46	
Depreciation office furniture	199.29	
Bonus to Shiell and Taylor	1,062.84	14,694.46
		$21,619.56
To—H. D. L. Gordon	$10,809.78	
—R. J. Dilworth	10,809.78	
		$21,619.56

This was indeed a creditable showing for ten months having regard to the short tenure of the partnership—five years and ten months—and particularly having regard to the value of the dollar in those days. The reference to Shiell and Taylor in the statement is to Robert Shiell and W. D. Taylor, two young Scottish accountants who joined in 1908 and who were later to become partners in the new firm.

The firm dissolved on January 31, 1913, and H. D. L. Gordon and R. J. Dilworth joined forces with the Clarksons.

Chapter 5

THE MERGER
CLARKSON, GORDON
& DILWORTH
1913

Early in 1913 Mr. G. T. Clarkson asked Mr. H. D. L. Gordon to come and see him, and he told Mr. Gordon that he would like him to take over the management of the accounting practice as Mr. Cross was about to retire. Mr. Gordon said "No" to this offer but said he would be glad to rejoin the Clarkson firm on the basis of full partnership provided Mr. R. J. Dilworth was offered the same terms. This proposal appealed to Mr. G.T. and a new partnership arrangement was promptly worked out. The new firm was to be known as Clarkson, Gordon & Dilworth, with E. R. C. Clarkson, G. T. Clarkson, H. D. L. Gordon, and R. J. Dilworth as partners, and it took over all the accounting practice of the

Clarksons, and of the old Gordon & Dilworth firm. As part of the agreement Gordon & Dilworth transferrred all their trustee and bankruptcy work to the Clarksons who then began to use the name E. R. C. Clarkson & Sons. In the latter firm the partners were Mr. E. R. C. Clarkson, and his three sons, G. T. Clarkson, Fred C. Clarkson, and E. Guy Clarkson.

The announcement sent to clients in 1913 is reproduced as Figure 4.

Messrs. Clarkson, Gordon & Dilworth
announce the formation of a partnership consisting of
E. R. C. Clarkson
G. T. Clarkson
H. D. Lockhart Gordon
R. J. Dilworth
to carry on as Chartered Accountants
the businesses formerly conducted by
Messrs. Clarkson & Cross and Messrs. Gordon & Dilworth

Toronto, 1st February 1913

Figure 4 THE 1913 ANNOUNCEMENT

Geoffrey Teignmouth Clarkson, eldest son of E. R. C. Clarkson, was born on October 21, 1878. He was educated at Model School and Jarvis Collegiate, and completed his formal education at the age of fifteen. Because he was too young to be accepted at University he decided to go to work and joined his father's firm in 1893. In business his two main specialties became bankruptcy work and the audit of chartered banks. Through the years he gained a wide reputation as trustee, liquidator, and assignee in a great many important business situations. Much of the method of bankruptcy practice, and indeed much of the legislation, has stemmed from principles established by Mr. G. T. Clarkson. He was the acknowledged expert on banks, and at one time was the auditor of five banks in Toronto—the Imperial, Toronto, Dominion, Metropolitan, and Standard. However, an amendment to the Bank Act in 1923 precluded a bank auditor from accepting special assignments from the banks, and it was necessary for him to resign his bank audits. He appeared on numerous occasions before the Senate Banking and Finance Committees dealing with periodic revisions of the Bank Act, and was considered an unusually useful witness.

In private life G.T. was rather shy and retiring, and his great love was the outdoors. As a youngster he had been granted a licence by the Province of Ontario to collect birds eggs, moths, fish life, etc., on Toronto Island "for scientific purposes," and he remained an ardent naturalist throughout his life. (His father, E. R. C. Clarkson, incidentally, not only had a cottage on what is now known as Centre Island, but also owned most of the island.) As a well-known gardener he collected rare species from all over the world, and his gardens in Wychwood Park were superb. G.T. loved fishing and duck shooting and his cottage in Muskoka. In the early days he and his brothers were highly respected aquatic competitors, and his main sport was paddling—when in training he used to paddle around Toronto Island. Throughout his life he maintained a keen interest in education. For many years, particularly through the depression years, he guided Havergal College as its Vice-Chairman of the Board, and was also Vice-Chairman of Wycliffe College and a Governor of Upper Canada College.

Mr. Clarkson died in 1949 in his seventy-first year. He had two sons, Robert C. Clarkson, the elder son, who before

Plate 6   G. T. CLARKSON

the war was with The Clarkson Company, and Geoffrey P. Clarkson, who is today a partner in the firm. Two of his grandsons are also with the firm, Geoffrey W. Clarkson (son of G. P. Clarkson) and Peter T. Bogart (son of G.T.'s eldest daughter). Plate 6 is a reproduction in colour of a portrait of Mr. G. T. Clarkson, done after his death by Cleeve Horne.

A reproduction of the Cleeve Horne portrait of Colonel Gordon, which was presented to him in 1951, is shown as Plate 7. Chapter 4 related very briefly something of his early background but this should be amplified. As a boy he had become keenly interested in sailing, and this was a sport he kept up after graduation until the time of his marriage. For a time he was a co-owner of a boat on Toronto bay which for a number of years won the annual race at the Royal Canadian Yacht Club. While at school H. D. L. Gordon was a good footballer and the year after graduating from R.M.C. actually played for Osgoode Hall, although how this was arranged is uncertain. Very early he took up riding and long before the First World War he was connected with the Toronto Mounted Rifles, which later became the Toronto Light Horse and finally the Mississauga Horse. For many years he kept his own horses until he stopped riding in 1950, and his favourite was "Buddy," a horse he rode for eighteen years. He also enjoyed both trout and salmon fishing which he took up seriously at about age 60.

At the time of declaration of war in 1914 Colonel Gordon was in command of the Mississauga Horse, and immediately went on active service. In 1914 the 4th Canadian Mounted Rifle Regiment was formed with units drawn from a number of others and he reverted to the rank of Major to assume command of "B" squadron and go overseas. He assumed command of the 4th C.M.R. in 1916, fought with distinction in many battles including Vimy Ridge, and was awarded a number of honours including the Distinguished Service Order (D.S.O.) and the Volunteer Officer's Decoration (V.D.).

He was wounded and returned to Canada in 1918 before the end of the war.

Colonel Gordon had a number of interests. For many years he was active in the Order of St. John of Jerusalem and for his good work was made a Knight of the Order in 1934. He has always been keenly interested in St. James' Cathedral and has taken an active part in its management, particularly its financial and investment affairs. Like his partners, G. T. Clarkson and R. J. Dilworth, he was greatly interested in the development of the profession, and served on the Council of the Ontario Institute, and as its President in 1933-34. However, it is probably safe to say that, next to his family, the Colonel's greatest interest is the practice. Until recent years he took close part in its management and for many years was the Senior Executive Partner. In business he was hard working, and provided the driving force for the firm in the years following the First World War. He also set high standards of professional conduct and had strict views of right and wrong in business practice.

H. D. L. Gordon had five brothers and three sisters, he being the eldest. One brother died from pneumonia at the age of twenty-six, another died in infancy, and two were killed in action in the First World War. His younger brother, Molyneux Gordon, will be remembered as a lawyer specializing in taxation and was first chairman of the Canadian Tax Foundation. The Colonel had three sons who joined him in the business. The eldest son is the Honourable Walter L. Gordon, for many years a senior partner and now Minister of Finance. His second son, Hugh Gordon, was killed in the Air Force in the Second World War; his third son, Duncan Gordon, is a partner in the firm today.

In the previous chapter a bit was said about the early days of R. J. Dilworth (whose picture appears as Plate 8), leading up to his joining Colonel Gordon in practice in 1906. At that time he was 37 years of age. Shortly after

Plate 7   H. D. L. GORDON

the formation of the new firm in 1913 the First World War broke out and Colonel Gordon went overseas, leaving R.J. with the entire burden of directing the accounting practice. In spite of his heavy work load, he found time to join a reserve unit of the Queen's Own Rifles (at that time he was 45) and qualified as a lieutenant. He was keenly interested in the profession, serving two terms as President of the Ontario Institute, and was one of the incorporators and first directors of the Canadian Society of Cost Accountants in 1920, the first meeting of the Society being held at 15 Wellington Street West. (It is now the Society of Industrial & Cost Accountants of Canada.) He did a lot of special work, was often called to court as an expert witness, and spent a great deal of time on the Canadian Customs Investigation.

R. J. Dilworth had an extraordinarily wide range of interests and hobbies outside of business. He was a great student of languages and taught himself German, Italian, French, and Spanish; he learned Spanish when he was about 70 years of age. At the time of his death, March 18, 1943, he had progressed to a point where he was reading *Don Quixote* in the original, and a copy was on his bedside table in the hospital. His hobbies included carpentry (he could make quite acceptable furniture), photography, sheet metal work, and copper beating. Mrs. Dilworth was a soprano of some distinction and the first to sing on a radio broadcast in Canada. It was R.J.'s interest in music that brought them together; he sang in the Mendelssohn Choir, where they met, and he himself occasionally performed as a baritone soloist. He also played the French horn and the 'cello. Like the Colonel, he was also a sailor, and in the summer when he lived on Toronto Island he would sail Mrs. Dilworth across to church on Sundays and she would sail him to work on week days. R.J. was a splendid golfer and the firm Challenge Cup is named for him. Not to be outdone by the children, at about the age of 70 he took swimming lessons in the Australian Crawl from Ernst Vierkotter. He had four children, two boys and two girls, and the eldest, Ralph W. E. Dilworth, is a partner in the firm today.

There can be no doubt that the most important single historical fact in the development of the firm, following its founding by Thomas Clarkson in 1864, was the decision of G. T. Clarkson, H. D. L. Gordon, and R. J. Dilworth to join together. Each of them was highly skilled and experienced in his profession, each was well known and respected by the business community, and each had his own wide circle of friends and acquaintances. It is difficult to imagine a more potent combination of attributes for a newly launched professional venture. They could have had no conception of how successful it was to be.

Plate 8   R. J. DILWORTH

Chapter 6

TWENTY-FIVE
YEARS OF GROWTH
1913-1938

The twenty-five year period following the formation of the new firms, Clarkson, Gordon & Dilworth, and E. R. C. Clarkson & Sons, in 1913
was one of great growth for the profession and
the firms. It was also a period that brought
troubled times, the First World War of 1914-18,
the recession of the twenties, and the great
depression of the early thirties. However, the
first fiscal year of the new operation was highly
successful and brought great promise for the
future. Fee revenue of the accounting practice
was substantially increased over the combined
revenue for the previous year of the Clarkson &
Cross and Gordon & Dilworth firms.

In the summer of 1914 H. D. L. Gordon went

overseas and was away until late in 1918. Robert Shiell, Harvey Guilfoyle, and Guy Clarkson also were away for the duration and the work load on the other partners was very heavy. Mr. R. J. Dilworth carried most of the burden as the senior partner on accounting work and Mr. G. T. Clarkson on trustee work and special assignments of various sorts. Principal members of the accounting staff during those years included W. D. Taylor and C. H. Pelling who had come from the Gordon & Dilworth firm, and C. A. Patterson and George F. Leaver who joined in 1917. Many graduates of the firm and some of the present staff will remember these men. W. D. Taylor had joined the Gordon & Dilworth firm in 1908, became a partner of the Clarkson, Gordon & Dilworth firm in 1921, and remained so until his death in 1940. He was a quiet unassuming person, and a splendid accountant for whom all had great admiration and affection, particularly the younger men who found him a helpful and willing teacher. C. H. Pelling had a wide reputation for his experience in mining accounting, and saw many of Ontario's great mining communities develop from original campsites. He retired from the firm in 1943 and died in 1947. C. A. Patterson, who joined in 1917, became a partner in 1935 and occupied a senior position in the firm at the time of his death in 1953. George Leaver, who also joined in 1917, became a partner in 1943 but left the firm three years later to assume an important post in business.

E. R. C. Clarkson & Sons in those early days had very few permanent employees, and staff was hired temporarily on a daily basis as the volume of trustee and bankruptcy work demanded. Mr. E.R.C. remained a partner until his death in 1931, but became less active through the years and his place as head of the firm was taken by Mr. G. T. Clarkson. Mr. Guy was away for the First World War but, apart from this, he and his older brother, Mr. Fred, worked with G.T. through this twenty-five year period. Fred Clarkson

Plate 9   THE BOARD ROOM AND MR. FRED CLARKSON

was born on December 3, 1880. He joined the firm in 1896 and was active until his death on August 6, 1951. Like G.T., Fred Clarkson was an outdoorsman and his particular love was trout fishing. He was a recognized expert on fishing, fish life, and fly tying, and was well known for his duck-shooting abilities. The three brothers were great paddlers, and Mr. Fred paddled to work from the Island in the summer. Mr. Fred spent two years on a lumbering venture in British Columbia with two of his brothers, working limits owned by the family, but this ended in a disastrous fire. Those who know the second floor board room at 15 Wellington Street today will be interested in Plate 9, which shows Mr. Fred seated at his old desk in that room. Mr. Guy Clarkson was born on January 7, 1888, was educated at Upper Canada College, and joined the firm in 1906 at the age of eighteen. He was a great athlete at school and after graduation developed into a football star and played on the championship Argonaut football team of 1912. He went overseas with the 123rd Battalion and won the Military Cross at Vimy Ridge. On returning from overseas he rejoined the firm and spent the remainder of his life there. He was also a naturalist, an enthusiastic gardener, and a good duck hunter, and loved his summer island in Muskoka. He was a member of the Board of Bishop Strachan School. Guy Clarkson died on June 21, 1960.

A younger brother, Maurice Clarkson, born in 1893, worked for a short time with the firm before the First World War. He was killed in action at Vimy Ridge.

The only permanent employee of the early days who played an important part with the Clarkson brothers was George S. Niven who joined them in 1914 and remained until his retirement in 1944. In addition to acting as senior employee for E. R. C. Clarkson & Sons, George Niven also did special work for the accounting firm, because he was particularly good at inventory problems and spotting operating inefficiencies in the plant.

As was to be the case also during the Second World War, the accounting work of the period 1914 to 1918 was affected materially by tax legislation of one kind or another. The Special War Revenue Act of 1915, the Business Profits War Tax Act of 1916, and the Income War Tax Act of 1917 all created their special problems for the taxpayers of Canada and their advisers. On his return from overseas in 1918 Colonel Gordon was quick to spot the continuing potential in special tax work and made sure the firm was equipped to handle it. Expansion continued and in 1921 three new partners were added, Robert Shiell, W. D. Taylor, and Harvey E. Guilfoyle, and in 1925 A. E. Nash.

In 1922 Robert Shiell, who had joined the Gordon & Dilworth firm in 1908, and had since become the brother-in-law of H. D. L. Gordon, moved to Montreal to open an office in the name of Clarkson, Gordon & Dilworth. Unfortunately he died suddenly in 1927 and it was necessary to make new arrangements for the Montreal practice. An approach was made to George C. McDonald and George Currie in Montreal who had been practising together since 1910, except for a period of service overseas in the First World War. Since the war these two first cousins, both good friends of H. D. L. Gordon and his partners, had built up a most satisfactory practice in Montreal and were well known and respected in the community. As of April 1, 1928, an arrangement was worked out under which the combined practice in Quebec and the Maritimes was to be carried out by the firm Clarkson, McDonald, Currie & Co., and in Ontario and the West by Clarkson, Gordon & Dilworth (which soon changed its name to Clarkson, Gordon, Dilworth, Guilfoyle & Nash). This continued until 1935, when the Montreal partnership was dissolved and each of the old firms reopened its own office in Montreal. During the period 1928 to 1935 each firm retained a good deal of autonomy but it was undoubtedly the hope that a large single firm would emerge. However, this was

Plate 10   H. E. GUILFOYLE

Plate 11   A. E. NASH

not to be, and the firms parted company with complete and continuing friendship. It is of interest to note that J. Grant Glassco, who had joined McDonald, Currie & Co. as a student in 1926, was loaned to the Toronto office in 1931 and stayed on to become a partner in Toronto in 1935.

The names of Harvey Guilfoyle and A. E. Nash (see Plates 10 and 11) were added to the firm name in 1928. Harvey Edward Guilfoyle was born in Lucan, Ontario, in 1887 and joined the firm of Gordon & Dilworth in 1912. He was keenly interested in the profession and, in addition to becoming President of both the Ontario Institute and the Dominion Association, he was also President of the Society of Industrial & Cost Accountants of Canada. During the First World War he served overseas as an officer in the 9th Mississauga Horse and returned to the firm in June of 1918, becoming a partner in 1921. Harvey Guilfoyle died suddenly at the age of 48, while on an assignment for the firm in New Brunswick in 1935. His son Harold Guilfoyle is a partner in the associated firm Woods, Gordon & Co.

Following the death of Mr. Guilfoyle in 1935 the name was changed to Clarkson, Gordon, Dilworth & Nash.

Albert Edward Nash was born in England in 1884 and was articled to a firm of chartered accountants before coming to Canada in 1907. He settled in Edmonton and began to practise as an accountant, shortly afterwards forming his own firm of Nash & Nash. In the First World War he enlisted as a private, and was commissioned with the 19th Alberta Dragoons. Overseas he was awarded the Military Cross and returned as a Major. After the war he decided to remain in Eastern Canada, and joined the firm in 1921, and became a partner in 1925. During the Second World War he was called up and appointed Assistant Adjutant and Quartermaster General of Military District No. 2 with rank of Lieut.-Colonel. He served in various successive posts such as Director of Organization in Ottawa with rank of Colonel, Deputy Adjutant-General with rank of Brigadier, Vice-Adjutant-General at National Defence Headquarters, and on May 16, 1944, he was appointed Inspector-General for Eastern Canada with rank of Acting Major-General. He died from a head injury on June 4, 1944. General Nash was a great administrator and a courageous soldier.

During this twenty-five year period four new offices were opened and two of these were later closed. Montreal was opened in 1922. In 1929 offices were opened in both Windsor and Ottawa. The Windsor office was primarily designed to provide local service to one large client and was closed in 1934. The Ottawa office was to provide contact in the federal capital, and was closed in 1937. An office was opened in Hamilton in 1938 which has continued to be one of the important Ontario offices of the firm.

It was a period of significant increase in work in spite of the depression period of the thirties. The firm was engaged on a considerable amount of regular audit work for various departments and commissions of the Ontario Government, and Mr. G. T. Clarkson in particular was doing a great deal of work for the chartered banks. The professional staffs of the two firms increased from about 15 in 1913 to about 115 in 1938. In the same period the total number of chartered accountants in Canada grew from 375 to 2,220. By 1938, only 63 per cent of these accountants were engaged in public practice and 37 per cent were in other pursuits, a clear indication of the way in which demand was growing for highly trained financial and accounting personnel in commerce and industry.

Of the eight partners in the accounting firm at the close of this period in 1938, only Colonel Gordon remains as a partner in 1964. Of the others, five have since died—W. D. Taylor (1940), R. J. Dilworth (1943), A. E. Nash (1944), G. T. Clarkson (1949), and C. A. Patterson (1953)—and two have retired, W. L. Gordon to become the Minister of Finance of Canada, and J. G. Glassco, President of

Brazilian Traction, Light and Power Company, Limited. Fortunately, four strong partners were admitted in the period 1939-41 who have remained with the firm until the present time, G. A. Adamson, G. P. Clarkson, G. G. Richardson, and J. R. M. Wilson. On the retirement of W. L. Gordon in 1963 Mr. Wilson assumed the chairmanship of the executive committee of Clarkson, Gordon & Co. and Mr. Clarkson assumed the similar post with Woods, Gordon & Co.

Chapter 7

THE WAR YEARS
1939-1945

The Second World War was particularly disruptive to all professional accounting firms. Traditionally their staff is made up for the most part of healthy young men between the ages of eighteen and thirty, and naturally the armed forces and government services relied heavily on intelligent young men of this sort. Some measure of the impact on the firm is provided by reference to the numbers involved. In 1939 the professional staff in the firm's three offices in Toronto, Montreal, and Hamilton numbered 139. During the war years 116 Clarkson, Gordon men and women served in the armed forces. A number of them did not return. Among the list of those killed on active service was Colonel Gordon's son Hugh

Gordon, and Grant Glassco's brother Hugh Glassco. Many will remember with great affection the firm's young office boy "Billy" Wallace, a Pilot Officer killed in action. One of the partners, Major-General A. E. Nash, died of a head injury received while making a routine inspection at Bowmanville, Ontario.

In addition to the service with the armed forces, many members of the firm contributed to important war work on the home front. Early in the war Walter Gordon went to Ottawa to assist in setting up the Foreign Exchange Control Board and later became a Special Assistant to the Deputy Minister of Finance. Grant Glassco was appointed by the Government as Controller and later Financial Administrator of Clyde Aircraft Limited at Collingwood which found itself in financial difficulties at a time when it was making urgently needed components for the Valentine Tank. Later he was appointed Controller of De Havilland Aircraft Company which was taken over by the Government. G. P. Clarkson went to New York to serve in the financial section of the British Purchasing Commission. Later he and Walter Gordon returned to spend full time with the J. D. Woods Company (see Chapter 10) which had been loaned to the Government to work for the Division for Simplification of Industry of the War Time Prices and Trade Board.

The problems of the firm, serious enough because of staff turnover, were compounded by the tremendous increase in special work which accompanied wartime conditions. Most important of this work was perhaps the preparation of briefs for submission to the Board of Referees under the Excess Profits Tax Act and, when necessary, appearing before that Board. The firm must have worked on over two hundred such briefs. Special assignments also arose out of various wartime orders, such as the Salary and Wage Control, Price Control, and the like, and special costing work under war contracts. This pressure accelerated the swing towards more reliance on test audit and internal control. It also forced the firm to employ young women as audit clerks.

The female staff, or L.A.C.'s as they were called (Lady Audit Clerks), worked out very well. The girls were intelligent and hard working and very quickly learned the fundamentals of auditing. To assist them the firm prepared a series of intensive lecture courses which were followed by written tests. These lectures, which proved very effective, were published in the *Chartered Accountant* magazine and later were made available to other practitioners in booklet form. There were about fifty such girls on the staff during the war and, as might have been expected, this large influx of attractive young women had a profound effect on the hitherto all male and dull routine at the office. A few of the girls attempted the C.A. course of instruction but only three carried on to graduate as chartered accountants, and they did exceptionally well. One of these was Miss Gertrude Mulcahy, a great-great-granddaughter of the founder of the firm, Mr. Thomas Clarkson. Her great-grandmother was Mr. Clarkson's first child Betsy, born in England in 1823 before he came to Canada.

Those who were on active service will recall, and perhaps with some nostalgia, the "Clarkson Dispatch." This was a mimeographed newsletter designed to keep the firm in touch with its men, and to keep them informed as to what was going on at home. The first issue came out in November 1941 as the "Clarkson War Cry," but was promptly renamed because one of the partners was concerned lest offence might be taken by a contemporary publication of similar name. The letter was originally intended to be produced monthly, or so the first issue boasted, but time and lack of news worked against this intention. In fact, there were only nine issues in all, the last being dated April 1945. In addition to keeping in close touch with the men in the services, the firm also purchased War Savings Certificates for them each month they were away.

During these years the firm grew moderately in size in spite of the difficulty in locating suitable personnel. No new offices were opened, however, until in 1945 an office was established in Vancouver. After the termination of the Clarkson, Cross & Helliwell firm, the firm had been represented in Vancouver but had not had its own office. Mr. W. Grant Ross moved from Toronto to Vancouver in 1945 to establish the practice in that city. One other very important milestone in the development of the firm during this period was the formation of the partnership of Arthur Young, Clarkson, Gordon & Co. The firm had enjoyed a long and friendly relationship with Arthur Young & Co. of the United States, and in 1944 the new joint firm was formed to conduct business in Canada for Arthur Young & Co. and in the United States for Clarkson, Gordon & Co.

Chapter 8

POST-WAR EXPANSION
1946-1963

Early in 1946 the name of the accounting firm was changed from Clarkson, Gordon, Dilworth & Nash to Clarkson, Gordon, & Co. and so it has remained. The name of E. R. C. Clarkson & Sons was changed at the same time to The Clarkson Company.

As mentioned in the previous chapter, there was only moderate growth in the firm through the war years, but in 1945 men began returning from overseas and numbers then increased rapidly. The period of 1946 to 1963 was one of very substantial growth in total numbers although in terms of percentage increase it was nothing like the expansion in the period 1913 to 1938.

At the beginning of 1946 the firm had four

offices, in Montreal, Toronto, Hamilton, and Vancouver, and a total staff of about two hundred, including administrative personnel, in the two Clarkson firms and the associated consulting firm of J. D. Woods & Gordon Ltd. At the end of this seventeen-year period there were twelve offices and the number of partners in the three firms had increased from 20 to 92 and the total staff from 200 to 900. A significant part of this growth resulted from a vigorous policy of extending service throughout the country, and took the form of mergers with other firms. The mergers and opening of new offices throughout this period are dealt with chronologically in following paragraphs.

1948 LONDON

In the summer of 1948 an office was opened in London, Ontario, with staff moved from Toronto. Initially it had an audit staff of six men and an administrative staff of two. In fifteen years it has had a remarkable growth and today is one of the firm's larger offices outside of Toronto.

1948 WINNIPEG

In the early days (1903) the firm had established the firm of Clarkson, Cross & Menzies in Winnipeg but this was terminated in 1913. Subsequently the firm had representation in Winnipeg until 1948, but in that year merged with the Winnipeg practice of Black, Hanson & Co. and opened an office in the firm name. Harold S. Hanson and A. H. Fisher became partners in the merged firm and continued in practice until their respective retirements.

1948 VANCOUVER

A Vancouver office had been established in 1897 by Clarkson, Cross & Helliwell which terminated in 1910, and the firm had reopened its own office again in 1945. In 1948 a merger was arranged with the local practice of Harold D. Campbell, who was not in robust health, and he continued for a time as a consultant with the firm.

1949 CALGARY

In 1917 Mr. Eric Richardson commenced public practice in Calgary, and in 1932 in association with Mervyn G. Graves he formed the firm of Richardson & Graves. That firm merged with Clarkson, Gordon & Co. on April 1, 1949, and continued its practice in Calgary with Mr. Graves as a partner in the firm and Mr. Richardson as a consultant.

1952 REGINA

Walter T. Read emigrated to Regina from England in 1913 and commenced to practise public accounting in his own name. After a period of service in the First World War he returned to form the partnership of Read, Smith & Co., which after a number of changes became Read, Smith & Forbes in 1943. On September 1, 1952, the firm merged with that partnership and W. T. Read, Ian Forbes, and W. E. Clarke became partners of Clarkson, Gordon & Co. (Mr. Frederick H. Smith had died in 1949). Mr. Read retired in 1957.

1955 LONDON

The London practice was merged in 1955 with that of Charles T. Sears who continued as a consultant with the firm until his death in 1961.

1956 EDMONTON

George Johnstone Kinnaird came from Dundee, Scotland, to Alberta in 1875. In 1910 he opened a public accounting practice specializing in municipal accounting. The practice was eventually taken over by his son G. D. K. Kinnaird after the latter's return from overseas in the First World War, and it eventually became Kinnaird, Aylen & Co. That firm merged with Clarkson, Gordon & Co. in 1956, with G. D. K. Kinnaird, B. G. Aylen, D. L. Brandell, J. M. Meikle, G. E. Pearson, and J. W. Stansberry becoming partners. Messrs. Kinnaird and Brandell have since retired from the firm and Messrs. Aylen and Stansberry have died.

1956 CALGARY

William Macintosh, who had trained with Messrs. Helliwell, Maclachlan in Vancouver, set up his own practice in Calgary with D. A. Ross in the firm Macintosh and Ross. In 1956 the partnership was dissolved and Mr. Macintosh joined Clarkson, Gordon & Co. bringing with him his personal practice. He continued as a partner of the firm until his retirement in 1961.

1957 WINDSOR

K. Douglas MacLennan trained in Windsor, Ontario, and from 1945 to 1951 he worked with firms of certified public accountants in Detroit. In 1951 he returned to Windsor to commence his own practice of public accounting which was merged with the firm in 1957, and Mr. MacLennan became a partner.

1959 VANCOUVER

The Vancouver firm of Carter, Reid & Walden merged with the firm on December 1, 1959, with A. M. Reid, F. E. Walden, and W. J. Smith becoming partners and G. W. J. Carter a consultant. This firm had been started by A. M. Reid in 1943, who was later joined by F. E. Walden. In 1948 they merged with G. W. J. Carter who had entered private practice in 1947 after leaving the position of Chief Assessor in the Vancouver district office of the Department of National Revenue.

1960 CALGARY

In October of 1960 the firm merged with Harvey, Morrison & Company, a substantial, well-established firm which had commenced practice in Calgary in 1924. K. J. Morrison (who retired in 1963), W. H. Nield, G. H. Jarman, and A. D. Stewart became partners.

1962 KITCHENER AND LONDON

In the early 1930's the late R. H. R. Brock commenced a private practice in Kitchener and was joined by D. Bruce

Davis in 1940. The firm eventually became Davis, Dunn and Broughton with offices in Kitchener and London, and the practice merged with that of Clarkson, Gordon & Co. in 1962. In the same year the partnership of Scully & Scully in Kitchener merged with the firm. This is a very old firm dating back to about 1850, and is of particular interest because it is the firm in which one of the senior partners of today, George G. Richardson, trained as a student. These mergers brought D. Bruce Davis, K. H. Dunn, John K. Broughton, and D. W. Scully into the firm partnership.

1962 QUEBEC

The firm achieved a long-cherished ambition in 1962 when it opened its own office in Quebec City and then a few months later entered into a merger with DeCoster, Normandeau & Cie. That firm was established in 1951 by Maurice DeCoster and Raymond and Yves Normandeau, who had previously practised with another firm. In 1954 Yves Normandeau left to become treasurer of the Quebec Catholic School Commission. At the time of merger in 1962 Maurice DeCoster retired to look after personal business interests and Raymond Normandeau became a partner in Clarkson, Gordon & Co.

In 1959 a new partnership was formed in Brazil. The Brazilian Traction companies have been audited by the firm for a great many years, The earliest report of which there is now a record is for the Sao Paulo Tramway, Light and Power Company, dated April 9, 1903, and signed by Clarkson & Cross. It reads as follows:

We have audited the books and accounts of the Sao Paulo Tramway, Light and Power Company at the Head Office in Toronto, Canada, from its inception in June, 1899, to 31st December, 1902, and hereby certify that all disbursements have been satisfactorily vouched and recorded. We have also audited the returns from the office at Sao Paulo of their operations, and

Plate 12   J. GRANT GLASSCO

find the result thereof to be correctly stated in the accompanying report.

With this important utility work as a base, the firm joined with Arthur Young & Co. and with Henry Martin & Co. of Uruguay to form the Brazilian partnership of Arthur Young, Clarkson, Gordon & Co., with offices in Rio de Janeiro and Sao Paulo.

Throughout this period the trustee work continued to grow in importance, and in 1954 the Clarkson Company partnership was dissolved and the business was transferred to a newly formed corporation, The Clarkson Company Limited.

The period of growth, 1946 to 1963, brought added strength to the firm with the addition of partners and staff from merged firms. The vigorous programme of expansion was initiated in large part by two senior partners who have since left the firm. While it was adopted as a definite policy of this historical sketch to refer in detail only to the partners of the early years, it would be an obvious mistake to omit reference to the parts played in the post-war period by J. G. Glassco and W. L. Gordon. These two outstanding accountants had a very wide circle of friends and acquaintances in business throughout Canada, which was of great importance to the firm.

John Grant Glassco (Plate 12), after graduation from McGill University, studied at the Sorbonne in Paris on a Province of Quebec scholarship. Upon his return to his home in Winnipeg he decided to obtain his c.a. degree as preparation for entering the utility business with the Detroit Edison Company which had offered him a job. His late father was also in the utility business, and at that time was General Manager of the Winnipeg City Hydro. Grant Glassco joined McDonald, Currie & Co. in Montreal in 1926 and in 1927 was moved to their Quebec City office where he remained until 1931. This was during the period of partnership with Messrs. McDonald and Currie, and Grant Glassco was sent to Toronto under an exchange arrangement which took Walter Gordon to Montreal. However, he stayed on in Toronto and remained with the Clarkson, Gordon firm, becoming a partner in 1935. While he earned a reputation as a tax specialist, he was a well-rounded accountant, with an international reputation as an accounting authority. His service to his profession was outstanding. In 1944 he was made a Fellow of the Institute, in 1948–49 was President of the Ontario Institute, and in 1954–55 was President of the Canadian Institute of Chartered Accountants.

J. G. Glassco's service during the war years is referred to in Chapter 7. In 1946 he was honoured by being made an officer of the Order of the British Empire. Since retiring from the firm in 1957 he has become President of Brazilian Traction, Light and Power Company, Limited, and is widely known as Chairman of the Royal Commission on Government Organization and author of "The Glassco Report." In private life he loves fishing, collecting stamps, and his farm at Woodbridge, where he experiments with Santa Gertrudis cattle developed on the King Ranch in Texas.

Colonel Gordon's son, Walter Lockhart Gordon (Plate 13), was educated at Upper Canada College and Royal Military College, Kingston, where he was an excellent athlete, both in track and football. In fact, after graduation he played for one year as a halfback with the Argonaut football team. He joined the firm in 1927. He became a partner in 1935 and from the start took an active interest in the management of the firm, eventually succeeding his father as the senior partner and remaining so until his retirement. He was instrumental in bringing together J. D. Woods & Co. Ltd. and Clarkson, Gordon in 1939 (see Chapter 10) and took over active direction of that firm in 1942, similarly remaining its head until his retirement in

Plate 13   WALTER L. GORDON

1963. It is safe to say that in the years following the First World War Walter Gordon was responsible more than any other single partner for setting the policies of both firms and providing the initiative which sparked their expansion. During his years with the firms he personally conducted or supervised an unusual number of special assignments and investigations of various kinds. He also headed up numerous royal commissions and special committees for the federal and Ontario governments. Of these, the outstanding one was, of course, the Royal Commission on Canada's Economic Prospects of 1955, which resulted in the famous "Gordon Report."

Walter Gordon's wartime service is referred to in Chapter 7. In 1946 he was honoured by being made a Commander of the Order of the British Empire. He always took a great interest in cultural and civic affairs and, amongst other things, was a President of the Board of Trade (1947), a Governor of the University of Toronto, and Chairman of the National Executive Committee of the Canadian Institute of International Affairs. Like his father, he is a fisherman and takes a keen interest in his farm at King, Ontario. In the general election of 1962 he was elected Liberal member for Toronto–Davenport. In 1963 he was re-elected and became Minister of Finance in the Federal Government and resigned from both the accounting and the consulting firms.

Through the period 1946 to 1963 the firm took advantage of a number of occasions to meet together with the former staff members (referred to always with affection as "the Old Boys"), to renew acquaintances and to relive the past. One such occasion was the dinner to honour Mr. G. T. Clarkson and Col. H. D. L. Gordon on their celebration of fifty years in practice. Plate 5 shows the three Clarkson brothers photographed together at that dinner. Another event which many will remember well is the reception held in 1951 at which the Cleeve Horne portrait of Colonel

Gordon (Plate 7) was presented to him. Those who attended will not forget seeing the Colonel standing before the portrait delivering his acceptance speech—a picture of this is shown in Plate 14, which illustrates better than words how perfectly Cleeve Horne has captured the character and spirit of the Colonel. In 1963 Colonel Gordon celebrated his ninetieth birthday. His partners presented him with 90 red roses and an illuminated salutation, a beautiful scroll in a leather cover, which read:

COLONEL H. D. LOCKHART GORDON,
D.S.O., V.D., K.ST.J., F.C.A.

On this the twentieth of July
in the year nineteen sixty-three
your seventy-four partners in
CLARKSON, GORDON & CO.,
join in saluting their senior partner
on his ninetieth birthday
and in extending
the warmest of good wishes
for the years ahead.

Plate 14   H. D. L. GORDON AND HIS PORTRAIT—1951

Chapter 9

GROWTH
OF THE PROFESSION

This is not the proper place to attempt a history of the profession in Canada, but in relating the history of the firm it does seem appropriate to make brief reference to the early beginnings of the professional societies in Canada and show how their membership has grown through the years.

When Mr. Thomas Clarkson commenced his practice as trustee and receiver in 1864, and when his son E.R.C. followed him in 1872, there were no organized accounting societies in Canada. The earliest accounting society in the world seems to have been formed in Scotland. In 1853 a group of accountants formed a voluntary association in Edinburgh and in 1854 a royal charter was granted under the name "The Society of Accountants in

Edinburgh." This was followed in 1855 by a charter for an institute of accountants in Glasgow and in 1867 by a charter for a society in Aberdeen. These later became part of the Institute of Chartered Accountants of Scotland. The Institute of Chartered Accountants in England and Wales was not incorporated until 1880, when it brought together a number of societies and institutes which had been formed in London, Liverpool, and other large centres from 1870 to 1880.

The Ontario Institute claims to be the oldest accounting body in Canada. A meeting was held in Toronto on November 11, 1879, by sponsors of an unincorporated society to be known as the "Institute of Accountants and Adjusters of Canada"; as mentioned in an earlier chapter, Mr. E. R. C. Clarkson was one of those sponsors. This organization later became the Institute of Chartered Accountants of Ontario which was incorporated by special act of the provincial legislature in 1883. The Ontario Institute appears to have preceded by just a few days the formation of an Association of Accountants in Montreal which held its first meeting on December 5, 1879. However, this latter association was much faster in obtaining the status of incorporation (1880), and was the first society to be incorporated in Canada, later becoming the Institute of Chartered Accountants of Quebec. In the early days it was apparently necessary to be examined for the degree of Fellow of the Ontario Institute. Among Mr. E. R. C. Clarkson's papers is a copy of his thesis read before the Institute Council as part of his examination on October 25, 1885.

Early in 1902 a group of practising accountants, not all of whom were members of one of the provincial institutes, announced their intention of applying to the Dominion Government for incorporation of a new Institute of Accounting, which would provide accounting education and instruction and would entitle its members to use the title "Chartered Accountant" anywhere in Canada. Apparently they also sought to preserve the title for the whole continent because an early draft of the proposed bill, found in Mr. E. R. C. Clarkson's papers, is entitled "An Act to incorporate the Institute of Chartered Accountants of North America." This proposed action alarmed some members of the provincial institutes (Ontario, Quebec, and Manitoba) who felt that confusion might result from having a number of separate accounting bodies each setting its own standards and granting the same degree. However, a measure of co-operation was worked out between the parties and the final bill omitted certain clauses which some provincial members found objectionable and made provision for admission to the new association (to be named the Dominion Association of Chartered Accountants) of the members of the various provincial institutes. The Dominion Association was incorporated on May 15, 1902, with Mr. E. R. C. Clarkson, Mr. W. H. Cross, and Mr. John F. Helliwell (then of Clarkson, Cross & Helliwell, Vancouver) amongst the twenty petitioners.

For some years the Dominion Association continued to admit members and permit them to use the designation of "Chartered Accountant," although the Ontario Institute attempted to prevent members of that association from practising as chartered accountants in Ontario. An act was passed by the Ontario legislature which reserved to the members of the Ontario Institute the right to use the designation "Chartered Accountant" in that province. The Dominion Association retaliated by obtaining an Order of Disallowance through the Dominion Government which blocked the provincial legislation. Relations between the bodies were less than cordial, but by the latter part of 1909 agreement was reached as to a future course for the profession in Canada. In 1910 amendments were made to the Dominion Association by-laws which resulted in its becoming the co-ordinating body for Canada. It then ceased to grant degrees and its members were given the right to admission to a provincial institute. Those who did not care to apply to a provincial institute were allowed to remain "members at large" of the Dominion Association. A later table shows seven such members in 1913, but all have since resigned or died. In 1951 the Dominion Association was renamed "The Canadian Institute of Chartered Accountants."

Over the years the growth in numbers of chartered accountants in Canada has been impressive, as illustrated by the following table.

ASSOCIATIONS OF CHARTERED ACCOUNTANTS, CANADA,
1913–1963

Date of incorporation	Society	1913 Membership	1963 Membership
1880	Quebec	61	3,233
1883	Ontario	144	5,274
1886	Manitoba	57	837
1900	Nova Scotia	21	206
1902	Dominion Association, Members at large	7	—
1905	British Columbia	38	1,113
1908	Saskatchewan	28	448
1910	Alberta	19	858
1918	New Brunswick	—	89
1921	Prince Edward Island	—	21
1949	Newfoundland	—	53
		375	12,132

This growth has been occasioned in large part by such things as the growing complexity of modern business finance, an increased participation by the public in the financing of business, government rules and regulations for control of such financing, a demand for greater disclosure of accurate information, and the intricate problems created by taxation of various sorts. The growth results in only small part from the growth in population over the last fifty years. A great many accountants are, of course, now employed in various aspects of trade and commerce, teaching, and governmental functions. Sixty years ago nearly every chartered accountant in Canada was engaged in public practice—today only one-half the chartered accountants are so engaged.

While the growth has been continuous through the years, it was substantially slowed down during the depression period of the thirties and during the Second World War. The following table shows the numbers at ten year intervals from 1910 to 1960.

Year	Number of chartered accountants	Increase over the ten-year period	Increase for the ten-year period expressed as a percentage
1910	255		
1920	570	315	124%
1930	1,440	870	153%
1940	2,422	982	68%
1950	3,939	1,517	63%
1960	9,107	5,168	131%

It is interesting to note that the increase in numbers from 1930 to 1940 was not significantly greater than the increase from 1920 to 1930. While in actual numbers the increase from 1940 to 1950 was much higher than from 1930 to 1940, the percentage increase was actually lower. Throughout the war years 1940 to 1945 the increase in numbers was very small, about three hundred for the whole period.

Over the last fifty years the profession has gained great stature. Members of the profession have worked hard to increase the standards in many directions. The quality of student instruction has been vastly improved and uniformity of basic training has been assured by standardization of examinations across the country. High standards of ethics have been set and have been diligently controlled, and in every direction the Canadian Institute has sought to improve the quality of performance, the extent of disclosure, and the value of the professional service to client and public alike. The firm has done its best to serve those ends. It has always adopted a policy of encouraging its members and staff to take full part in all work of the institutes and their various committees. In fact, the firm has recognized its serious obligation, as a large well-established member of the profession, to accept its full share of responsibility for development of the profession. It would not be practicable to attempt to list all the men who, over the years, have accepted major responsibility on institute councils, in standing and special committees, or in special tasks from time to time. However, a good indication of the firm's contribution is given by the following list of partners who have served as presidents of the Canadian and provincial institutes:

Term	Institute	
1887–88	Ontario	E. R. C. Clarkson
1904–05	Canadian	W. H. Cross
1919–20	Ontario	R. J. Dilworth
1920–21	Ontario	R. J. Dilworth
1930–31	Alberta	K. J. Morrison
1933–34	Ontario	H. D. L. Gordon
1934–35	Alberta	G. D. K. Kinnaird
1935 (died Oct. 14/35)	Canadian	H. E. Guilfoyle
1940–41	Alberta	M. G. Graves
1942–43	Alberta	B. G. Aylen
1942–43	British Columbia	W. A. Macintosh
1945–46	Ontario	C. A. Patterson
1948–49	Ontario	J. G. Glassco
1950–51	Canadian	K. J. Morrison
1950–51	British Columbia	W. G. Ross
1954–55	Canadian	J. G. Glassco
1955–56	Alberta	W. H. Nield
1956–57	Saskatchewan	Ian Forbes

Term	Institute	
1956-57	Ontario	J. R. M. Wilson
1957-58	Quebec	G. P. Keeping
1959-60	British Columbia	F. E. Walden
1960-61	British Columbia	D. B. Fields
1961-62	Alberta	D. A. McGregor
1963-64	Ontario	D. L. Gordon
1964-65	Quebec	H. M. Caron
1964-65	Saskatchewan	W. E. Clarke

Chapter 10

WOODS, GORDON & CO.

The story of the firm would not be complete without a brief history of the Woods, Gordon firm. In addition to serving its own important clients, the consulting firm provides management services for the clients of the accounting firm, and the two work closely together.

Woods, Gordon & Co. had its origin in the timestudy department of the York Knitting Mills Limited, Toronto. Back in the late 1920's, the Charles E. Bedaux Co., one of the early firms of American industrial engineers, came to Toronto and persuaded Mr. J. Douglas Woods, President of York Knitting Mills, that they could reduce direct labour costs substantially by introducing a wage incentive plan based on produc-

Plate 15　J. DOUGLAS WOODS

Plate 16   RALPH PRESGRAVE

tion standards set by timestudy. The Bedaux engineers worked for two years installing the wage incentive plan, and during that time trained Ralph Presgrave, a York executive, to carry on after they left. Through the years Ralph Presgrave became a recognized international authority in the field of industrial engineering. He made certain modifications in both the Bedaux wage incentive plan and the timestudy system on which it was based, modifications that he considered to be improvements. He also built up a staff of industrial engineers to assist in extending the wage incentive plan to a group of additional textile plants that the York Knitting Mills had acquired in Hamilton and Woodstock.

By 1932 it was believed that the techniques developed at York Knitting Mills were at least equal to anything being offered by American firms of industrial engineers and that there was a place for a purely Canadian firm in the field. Accordingly it was decided to incorporate J. D. Woods & Co. Ltd. and to take on work outside the York Knitting Mills. Mr. J. D. Woods (Plate 15) was the President of the company; Ralph Presgrave (Plate 16) was the Vice-President; E. D. MacPhee was the Managing Director (he was also General Manager of York Knitting Mills at that time and has since retired from the post of head of the Department of Commerce and Business Administration at the University of British Columbia); V. W. T. Scully was the Secretary-Treasurer (he was a Clarkson, Gordon & Co. graduate who was comptroller of York Knitting Mills at the time and is now President of the Steel Company of Canada); A. W. Baillie, now President of Bowes Company Limited, was a director; J. A. Lowden and D. M. Turnbull who joined the Woods firm as members of the original group have continued as partners to the present time.

During the 1930's, J. D. Woods & Co. Ltd. continued to do a good deal of work in the various plants of the York Knitting Mills, but gradually it took on more and more outside assignments, first in the textile industry, where the staff had had previous experience, and then in a wider range of industries, particularly those engaged in metal working. The company also became more diversified in its activities. Initially, the main service offered to clients consisted of training a group of timestudy men and helping them set up wage incentive plans and labour controls. Gradually, however, the company broadened its activities in the industrial engineering field and took on assignments in the systems and procedures field and the sales and merchandising field. Throughout the thirties, however, the group was a small one, never numbering more than a dozen men.

The association with Clarkson, Gordon & Co. started in 1939. By that time it had become apparent that the accounting firm was getting into more and more business problems on behalf of its clients that were only indirectly connected with accounting and financial matters, and that sooner or later it would be necessary to obtain staff with a wide range of skills or join forces with an existing organization that had such skills. The two groups decided to join forces, and a new company, The J. D. Woods Co. Limited, was set up. W. L. Gordon, J. G. Glassco, and C. A. Patterson represented the accounting firm on the board of directors and J. D. Woods, W. B. Woods, and Ralph Presgrave represented a group known as Woods Bros. & Associates. Because of the outbreak of war, the two groups continued to operate separately. The Woods group handled all the production and merchandising services from their office in the York Knitting Mills, and a small group in the auditing firm handled the systems and procedures services from 15 Wellington Street West.

By 1942, enlistments in the armed forces had reduced the staff to a mere handful, but in that year W. L. Gordon conceived the idea of placing the entire firm at the disposal of the Government to aid in its programme of conserving manpower and materials. He took over active direction of the firm, space was rented in the Star Building on King Street in Toronto, and the staff was expanded from a nucleus of about five men to a total of over thirty. During 1942 and 1943 the firm undertook a wide variety of studies on behalf of the Canadian Government. This work came to an end late in 1943, and the next year the firm of J. D. Woods & Gordon Ltd. was formed and took up offices with the accounting firm at 15 Wellington Street West. Only a few of those who had worked for the Government were retained, and once again the firm faced the task of building up its staff. The first board of directors was composed of J. D. Woods as President, W. L. Gordon as Managing Director, Ralph Presgrave, J. G. Glassco, J. A. Lowden, G. P. Clarkson, D. M. Turnbull, and B. H. Rieger.

During the post-war years there was a growing demand for consulting services, and this period saw a corresponding growth in the consulting staff. It soon numbered about forty and was maintained around this level throughout the 1950's. The same period saw an increase in the variety and scope of assignments undertaken and in the types of clients served. The firm continued to provide extensive services in the production field, and equipped itself to meet the growing demand for organization studies, marketing surveys, economic forecasts, wage and salary surveys, management control procedures, data processing systems, and so on. The firm also moved beyond the strictly business world and accepted assignments for government at all levels, hospitals, professional associations, and educational institutions.

As the firm changed, so did its corporate structure. J. D. Woods became Chairman of the Board and W. L. Gordon became President, and the number of directors, originally eight, more than doubled. On January 1, 1959, the firm ceased to be a limited company and became a partnership. At that time Mr. J. D. Woods and Mr. Ralph Presgrave retired and became consulting partners. Today the firm comprises some sixty men, including partners, senior consultants and consultants, and it shares offices with Clarkson, Gordon & Co. in Montreal, Toronto, London, Calgary, and Vancouver. The very close relationships that have built up between the partners and staff of the two firms provide the basis for bringing their combined skills to bear on the problems of their clients.

Chapter 11

15 WELLINGTON WEST

The firm has now occupied 15 Wellington Street West since April 1, 1913, or for a little more than fifty years. No present or former partner or staff member, except Colonel Gordon, is likely to remember any of the earlier locations. Actually there were relatively few changes of address over the years considering the rapid change and growth both in the city and in the firm itself. Most of the prior locations were very close to, and all were within a very few blocks of, the present office building. Several of them were on Wellington Street, which was originally Market Street and was renamed for Arthur Wellesley, Duke of Wellington, as were a number of other streets, crescents, and avenues in Toronto. Jordan

Figure 5   THE EXCHANGE BUILDING

Street, at the foot of which lies the present building, was named after a famous old Toronto clockmaker, Jordan Post, who at one time owned the whole of the south side of King Street between Yonge and Bay Streets. One block to the north is Melinda Street, which was named after his wife.

Figure 6   WELLINGTON STREET—1870

Mr. Thomas Clarkson opened the first office at 83 Front Street East in 1864—this old building still stands just to the west of St. Lawrence Market. He remained there for five years, and then the firm moved to the Exchange Building (Fig. 5). This building stood at the northwest corner of Wellington Street and Leader Lane, which was originally known as Berczy Street; this corner had been the site of the sixth post office prior to its removal to the west side of Toronto Street (now the head office of Argus Corporation) and Mr. Berczy had been the postmaster. The Exchange Building was an early meeting place of the Toronto Board of Trade. In 1877 it was taken over and substantially altered by the Imperial Bank as its head office.

The Clarkson firm then moved to 44 Front Street West (1878–1881) and then to 17 Toronto Street (1882). In 1883 it moved back to Wellington Street East to No. 26, very close to its old location in the Exchange Building. Figure 6 shows Wellington Street looking west from Leader Lane in 1870. Not shown in the picture, immediately to the right of "R. Jordan & Co.," stood the old Exchange Building. Down the street to the left of Molson's Bank is No. 26, a small yellow clapboard cottage occupied in 1870 by a Mr. Campbell, boot maker. By 1883 the cottage at No. 26 had been replaced by a handsome new structure, the North British and Mercantile Insurance Company Building, which still stands at that address.

In 1896 the firm moved from 26 Wellington Street East next door to the Ontario Bank Building at the corner of Wellington and Scott streets. Its address became "Ontario Bank Chambers, 33 Scott Street." This fine old building which was built in 1862 is still standing, but the property is now for sale and it is feared that it may be torn down. The Wellington Street entrance of the Ontario Bank can be seen in Figure 6 just to the left of the little cottage (No. 26). A pen sketch of the Scott Street façade is shown as Figure 7. The accounting firm remained in the Ontario Bank Chambers until the merger of the Clarksons with H. D. L. Gordon and R. J. Dilworth in 1913. The E. R. C. Clarkson trustee and receivership business remained for a few months at the old location, primarily because Mr. G. T. Clarkson was at that time winding up the affairs of the Ontario Bank and it was convenient for the firm to be

Figure 7   33 SCOTT STREET

located close to the Bank's records and particularly to be able to use the Bank's board room.

When Colonel Gordon left Messrs. Clarkson and Cross to establish his own practice in 1905 he moved to 186 York Street in the Penny Bank offices, and R. J. Dilworth joined him there in 1906. In 1911 the Gordon and Dilworth firm, having outgrown that space, moved to new quarters in the Lumsden Building at the northeast corner of Adelaide and Yonge. On April 1, 1913, the newly merged firm of Clarkson, Gordon & Dilworth moved to 15 Wellington Street West (Fig. 8), where it took over the top floor.

The building was designed by William Thomas, architect, and was erected for the Commercial Bank of the Midland District (which became the Commercial Bank of Canada in 1856) in 1843 or 1845. Professor Eric Arthur, Chairman of the Committee on Preservation of Historic Buildings of the Royal Architectural Institute of Canada,

Figure 8   15 WELLINGTON STREET WEST

was good enough to send the firm a copy of the following
note written in 1867 which he had found amongst some
old papers:

Commercial Bank of Canada, built in 1845, of Queenston stone,
from designs by the late William Thomas architect, at a cost
of £4,584. The land cost £2,271, 14s, but from this is to be
deducted £1,280 received from two lots sold off, thus reducing
the cost to £991, 14s.

Cost of building	18,336 $
Cost of land	3,967 $
	22,303

Toronto, Feb. 20, 1867

The firm has framed in its foyer an attractive set of
drawings of the building, which are reproduced as Figures 9
and 10. These are scaled measured drawings of the northern

Plate 17   THE MERCHANTS BANK

façade and show enlarged details of the principal items of design and ornamentation, and one of the many fireplaces. These measured drawings were done by Mr. Leonard E. Shore (now senior partner in the firm of architects, Shore & Moffat) in 1932, as part of a study of historic buildings sponsored by the University of Toronto under the direction of Professor Eric Arthur.

Messrs. William Thomas & Sons were prominent architect-engineers of the day. William Thomas was born in Stroud in 1800, and his training, like that of John G. Howard (who in 1836 built Colborne Lodge as his family estate, which still rests intact in Toronto's High Park), was such as to produce the architect-engineer. In fact in 1853 he was appointed City Engineer of Toronto. William Thomas was the designer of many fine old Toronto buildings, including St. Michael's Cathedral and St. Lawrence Hall. The latter was built in 1850 after the great fire of 1849 and once served as City Hall and a major cultural centre of Toronto. In an earlier chapter reference is made to meetings in the Hall attended by Mr. Thomas Clarkson. It is expected that St. Lawrence Hall will be restored and renovated as part of the centenary celebration of 1967. In an article in its issue of December 10, 1963, the *Toronto Daily Star*, with the advice of four historians and architects, selected ten old Toronto structures worth saving. This list included 15 Wellington Street West, the Ontario Bank Building (the firm's former premises at the corner of Wellington and Scott streets), St. Lawrence Hall, the old post office at 10 Toronto Street, now the home office of Argus Corporation, and Colborne Lodge referred to above.

Long before the firm moved into 15 Wellington West, the building had changed hands. The Commercial Bank of Canada failed in the year 1868, and was taken over by the Merchants Bank of Canada in that year, and Plate 17 is a picture of the building with the latter bank's sign prominently displayed across the front. In 1922 the Mer-

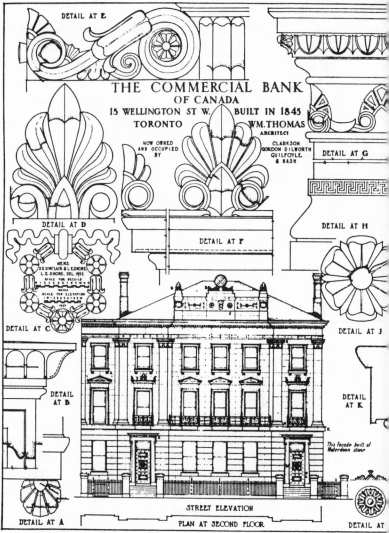

Figure 9 DRAWING BY LEONARD E. SHORE

chants Bank of Canada was taken over by the Bank of Montreal.

When the Clarkson, Gordon and Dilworth firm moved to 15 Wellington West on April 1, 1913, there were two entrances. One door, to the east (No. 13), was the entrance to the Banking Chambers, and the other (No. 15), was originally the entrance to the Bank Manager's apartment.

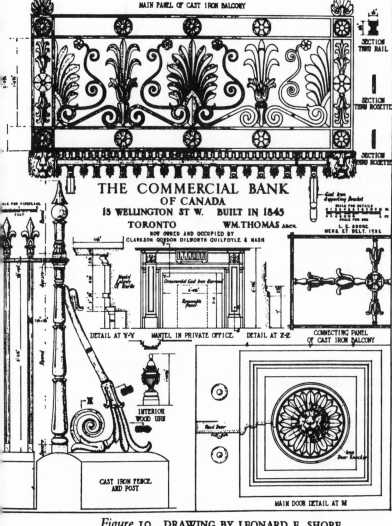

Figure 10   DRAWING BY LEONARD E. SHORE

He had living and dining rooms on the second floor and
bedrooms on the third floor. Originally most of the rooms
throughout the building had beautiful fireplaces, but all
except three have since been removed in the course of
successive alterations. At the back of the building there was
a nice garden which was still there in the early 1930's, and
at the end of the lot stood a stable and coach house.

By 1920 the firm's business had expanded substantially and more space was required. The Merchants Bank was anxious to move to King Street and was therefore interested in selling the building. H. D. L. Gordon and R. J. Dilworth went to Montreal to negotiate the purchase with L. C. Macarow, General Manager of the Merchants Bank. Old notes of the trip suggest that a spirited process of bargaining took place, with the end result that the Bank's asking price of $137,500 was negotiated downwards to a settlement at $112,500, the figure which appears in the firm's books of account, of which $40,029 was attributed to the land. The agreement of purchase is an interesting document and reflects the high opinion the vendors held of the ingenuity and ambitions of the purchasers, for it expressly provided: "Purchaser agrees as a condition of this purchase that they will not use or permit the said premises to be used for banking purposes." The description of the property refers to the 999-year lease dated 1882 covering the lane to Front Street and provides for free and uninterrupted use for "carts, vehicles, carriages, horses or cattle as by them should be convenient at all times and seasons."

Ten years after acquisition it was necessary to extend the building and in 1930-31 an "annex" consisting of a basement and three floors was added to the west end at the rear, running south towards Front Street. Ten years later in 1941 the fourth floor was added to the first annex. This annex was very quickly outgrown, and immediately after the war a second two-storey annex was added, running east and west across the rear. The two-storey addition (completed 1946) was extended to four floors in 1953.

By 1960 the quarters had again become quite inadequate, and the administrative and internal accounting functions had been moved into rented quarters across the street. Serious consideration was then given to long-term space requirements and it was necessary to make a difficult decision as to whether or not the old location should be given up. It was finally agreed that the old building should be retained and renovated, and that adjacent land to the west should be acquired for immediate and long-term expansion.

In the course of examining the building and planning the renovation the architects became concerned about a number of unusual faulting cracks in the walls and ceilings and, as a result, structural engineers were engaged to make a thorough exploration of its condition by opening holes in walls, floors, and ceilings throughout. This exploration revealed serious weaknesses which required immediate temporary support timbers to be installed, particularly in the big room on the main floor. An application to the City of Toronto for a permit to proceed with a new addition while occupying the old building in a temporarily reinforced condition resulted in a further examination by city inspectors. The application was not only refused but the building was condemned and the firm was ordered to vacate. In February of 1960 the Woods, Gordon and the Clarkson Company firms moved into temporary quarters in the old Bank of Nova Scotia Building on Melinda Street, and the Clarkson, Gordon firm was compressed into the annex structures.

The adjacent land was acquired and work commenced immediately on a four-storey addition to the west, which is so planned that it can form a part of successive major additions in the future. Most of the present staff in Toronto, and many friends and clients, will recall the chaos and confusion which ensued, and the problem of getting into the annex through the protective front hall tunnel, all reminiscent of wartime bomb damage. The work was tricky because of the condition of the support structures, and even removal of the old banking insignia on top was a delicate manoeuvre. This stone-work was referred to in Nelson's *Handbook of Toronto* for 1860 as "an enriched parapet surmounted by a globe." It was found, on inspection, that the tremendously heavy stone globe was in a precarious state, held in position only by a metal pin which had become thoroughly corroded over the years. This was carefully removed by a mobile crane of the Frankel Steel Construction Company working from the street, anxiously supervised by Mr. Frankel himself lest it might go crashing through all three floors.

The new addition ties in well with the old building, resulting in a centre hall structure for the four floors of the original annex addition. The new space is air-conditioned and comfortable and internally blends well with the old structure. On the outside the entrance is set well back so that the new construction does not detract significantly from the handsome façade of Mr. William Thomas' 1845 Greek design. Ownership of the parking lot has been retained to permit further expansion if and when required. A pen sketch of the building in its present form has been made for the firm by a Canadian artist, G. H. Mills, o.s.a., a.r.c.a., and a copy of it is reproduced as Plate 18.

A good indication of the way in which costs have risen and the value of the dollar has decreased is given by the following table of expenditures on the land and building over the years:

		LAND	BUILDING
1845	Original cost to the Commercial Bank of the Midland District	$ 3,967	$ 8,336
1920	Purchase of the original property by the firm from the Merchants Bank	40,029	$ 72,471
1930–31	First annex, basement and three floors		$ 43,800
1941	Fourth-floor addition to first annex		$ 21,289
1945–46	Second annex, basement and two floors		$ 69,805
1953	Two-floor addition to second annex		$101,380

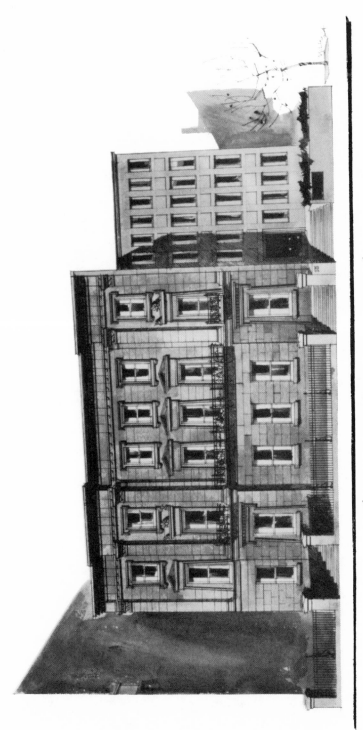

Plate 18   15 WELLINGTON STREET WEST—1964

1960–61 Acquisition of land to the west,
including parking lot, and
four-storey addition to building with structural tie-in and
renovation of old premises $423,782 $615,452

In the note received from Professor Arthur mentioned earlier, reference is made to certain land which was sold off by the Commercial Bank in 1845 for £1,280 ($5,120). It is interesting to speculate as to whether or not this might be the same property which the firm bought back in 1960 for $423,782!

Chapter 12

1964

The year 1964 brings to a close the first one hundred years in the development of the firm. The changes throughout this period were immense, not only because the change in the pattern of business finance and development was great, but particularly because the profession was virtually non-existent in Canada a hundred years ago. Mr. Thomas Clarkson would be amazed to find that the little town of York with 8,000 inhabitants, to which he came in 1832, had developed into a bustling metropolitan community of some 1,700,000 persons. He would probably be even more amazed by the variety of services offered to the clients today.

As part of the centenary celebrations in honour

of its founders, the firm plans to have anniversary dinners or receptions in a number of cities across Canada in the Fall of 1964. It is hoped that as many of the graduates as possible will be able to attend one of them. In appendixes attached there are listed the names of all the former personnel of Clarkson, Gordon & Co., Woods, Gordon & Co. and The Clarkson Company Limited for whom the firms have adequate records. All of these people will, of course, be invited to attend. There are also listed for the historical record all the members of the staff of the firms. Because of physical problems of publication it unfortunately has been necessary to close the lists as of July 1, 1964, so that subsequent staff changes, or changes of position, cannot be included.

In honouring the founding partners in 1964, all the present partners are conscious of the debt they owe these men for their courage and foresight in developing the firms, for their wisdom in setting standards and determining policies, and above all for their practice of transferring responsibility to the younger men as quickly as they could assume it. How well these lessons have been learned remains to be told at some future celebration one hundred years from now.

APPENDIXES

APPENDIX I

DECEASED, RETIRED AND FORMER PARTNERS OF THE CLARKSON, AND CLARKSON GORDON FIRMS
(showing dates of partnership in the firm)

DECEASED PARTNERS

Thomas Clarkson	1864–1872	E. G. Clarkson	1913–1960
E. R. C. Clarkson	1870–1931	Robert Shiell	1921–1927
Thomas Munro	1872–1877	H. E. Guilfoyle	1921–1935
John Turner	1877–1881	W. D. Taylor	1921–1940
W. H. Cross	1891–1913	A. E. Nash	1925–1944
G. T. Clarkson	1905–1949	C. A. Patterson	1935–1953
R. J. Dilworth	1907–1943	J. W. Stansberry	1956–1960
F. C. Clarkson	1913–1951	B. G. Aylen	1956–1963

RETIRED AND FORMER PARTNERS

J. G. Glassco	1935–1957	W. B. Coutts	1954–1956
W. L. Gordon	1935–1963	G. D. K. Kinnaird	1956–1958
J. C. Thompson	1939–1941	R. R. Jackson	1956–1961
G. F. Leaver	1943–1946	L. F. Stevens	1956–1962
H. S. Hanson	1948–1953	D. L. Brandell	1956–1963
A. H. Fisher	1948–1958	W. A. Macintosh	1957–1961
J. H. Moore	1950–1953	E. H. Orser	1958–1961
W. T. Read	1952–1957	T. G. Sheeres	1959–1961
D. I. Webb	1953–1955	K. J. Morrison	1960–1963
R. H. Ellison	1953–1956	Edward Stamp	1961–1962

APPENDIX II

FORMER PERSONNEL OF CLARKSON, GORDON &
CO. AND THE CLARKSON COMPANY LIMITED,
AND THEIR POSITIONS AT JULY 1, 1964

J. H. A'Court 1937–1947
Vice-President, Finance,
Brazilian Traction, Light and Power Company, Limited

C. Fred Adams 1936–1941
Accountant, Savage Shoes Limited

E. C. Adams 1949–1960
Manager, Profit Analysis,
Ford Motor Company of Canada, Limited

A. M. Adamson 1935–1946
Vice-President and General Manager,
Canadian General-Tower Limited

W. R. Aird 1948–1954
Treasurer & Comptroller,
Pulp & Paper Research Institute of Canada

John C. Aldred 1947–1960
Fidelity Mortgage and Savings Corporation

K. G. Allaster 1955–1959
Assistant Treasurer, Delta Acceptance Corporation Limited

Kenneth E. Allen   1926-1932
Financial Administrator,
Connaught Medical Research Laboratories, University of Toronto

Loftus A. Allen   1912-1914
Partner, Loftus A. Allen & Co., Chartered Accountants

Peter H. R. Alley   1952-1963
Controller, R. Laidlaw Lumber Co. Limited

J. M. Allison   1923-1929
Retired

Philip J. Ambrose   1939-1947
Sheriff, County of York

A. R. G. Ament   1928-1936
Treasurer, Brazilian Traction, Light and Power Company, Limited

Robert L. Anderson   1954-1962
Investigation Auditor, Law Society of Upper Canada

A. Arnold Anglin   1931-1936
Manager,
Membership Department, Sarasota County Chamber of Commerce

Hugh W. Archibald   1952-1953
Director & General Manager, Lastex Yarn & Lactron Thread Ltd.

T. Ross Archibald   1958-1962
Research Assistant (Ph.D. Student),
Graduate School of Business, University of Chicago

William P. Armes   1949-1952
Energy Returns Officer, Ontario Energy Board

R. Armitage   1947-1956
Comptroller, John Inglis Co. Limited

David G. Armstrong   1959-1963
In practice with
Arthur Young, Clarkson, Gordon & Co.,
Accountants & Auditors

Robert A. Armstrong   1931-1935
Partner, Armstrong, Browne & Co., Chartered Accountants

Gordon V. Ashworth   1945-1953
Treasurer and Controller, Telegram Publishing Co. Limited

G. J. Aubrey   1957–1962
Secretary-Treasurer, Seiberling Rubber Co. of Canada, Ltd.

Yves Aubry   1956–1961
Trésorier, Distributeurs Delorimier Distributors Inc.

Eliot M. Auger   1943–1952
Vice-President, Finance and Administration,
Canadian Motorola Electronics Company

F. A. Axon   1940–1953
Director,
Gasoline Tax Branch, Treasury Department, Province of Ontario

J. Ross Backus   1944–1950
Business Administrator & Secretary-Treasurer,
The Board of Education of the City of Oshawa

D. Gordon Badger   1955–1964
Vice-President, John Caisley & Company Limited

G. D. Bailey   1935–1939
Secretary-Treasurer, John Clark Building Enterprises

Irwin A. Bailey   1934–1939
Vice-President & General Manager,
Southern Division, Moore Business Forms Inc.

R. L. T. Baillie   1946–1957
Comptroller,
North American Operations, Massey-Ferguson Limited

Stuart H. R. Bain   1954–1957
Partner, Peat, Marwick, Mitchell & Co., Chartered Accountants

O. Perry Baird   1958–1962
—

Ralph Banner   1951–1960
Staff Consultant, Canadian Westinghouse Co. Ltd.

Russell Barker   1958–1962
Assessor, Department of National Revenue

Robert A. Barr   1950–1954
Partner, Peat, Marwick, Mitchell & Co., Chartered Accountants

Peter Bass   1948–1955
Partner, A. W. Jackson & Co., Chartered Accountants

J. Robert Bateman   1949–1954
Partner, Gunn, Roberts & Co., Chartered Accountants

D. C. Beacom   1953–1959
Assessor, Taxation Division, Department of National Revenue

William E. Beacom   1952–1955
Manager, Systems & Audit, Imperial Oil Limited

W. R. Beacom   1947–1951
In practice, W. R. Beacom, Chartered Accountant

Brian G. Beatty   1957–1962
Internal Auditor, Canadian National Railways

Bruce H. Becker   1951–1952
Manager, Group Underwriting, Confederation Life Association

J. E. Beckett   1943–1946
In practice, J. E. Beckett, Chartered Accountant

Gordon A. Beese   1945–1952
Disbursements Supervisor,
Hydro-Electric Power Commission of Ontario

George H. Beeston   1913–1923
President, General Theatre Investment Company Limited

Norman H. Beiles   1956–1963
Partner, Fox, Beiles & Co., Chartered Accountants

D. S. Bell   1947–1955
Assistant Secretary-Treasurer, Sinclair Canada Oil Co.

Leon Bennet-Alder   1944–1948
Administrator, Miners Clinics, Inc.

A. K. Bennett   1953–1959
Financial Analyst, Polymer Corporation Ltd.

Peter M. L. Bennett   1950–1961
Comptroller, Gibson Bros. Limited

R. C. Bertram   1929–1934
Partner,
Riddell, Stead, Graham & Hutchinson, Chartered Accountants

A. R. Bethell   1951–1956
Methods Analyst, City of Vancouver

G. L. Bingleman 1954–1962
Co-ordinator, Government Accounting,
Canadian Westinghouse Company Limited

Francis Gerard John Black 1948–1951
Assistant Comptroller, Canadian National Railways

Earl Blaine 1954–1958
Assistant Professor,
Faculty of Commerce, University of British Columbia

J. M. Blanch 1934–1944
Treasurer, Charles E. Frosst & Co.

D. H. Blanchard 1952–1956
Comptroller, Provincial Motor Clubs Limited

Marcel G. Blanchet 1957–1960
In practice with
Arthur Young, Clarkson, Gordon & Co., Accountants & Auditors

R. Paul Boddy 1945–1953
Vice-President, General Concrete Ltd.

Ernest C. Bogart 1945–1946, 1948–1951
President, Diversified Credit Corporation Ltd.

N. T. Boleychuk 1959–1962
Controller, Edmonton Exhibition Association Ltd.

Mary Bond 1920–1962
Retired

Bruce C. Bone 1951–1957
Treasurer, Kerr Addison Mines Limited

Gordon H. Boody 1940–1950
Comptroller,
Canada Brick Division, Martin-Marietta (Canada) Limited

Douglas R. Booz 1952–1957
Assistant Chief Accountant, North York Board of Education

William H. Boulding 1949–1953
Office Manager, Interprovincial Steel & Pipe Corp. Ltd.

Basil J. Bouris 1954–1959
Partner,
Bouris, Wilson, Scott, Robinson & Co., Chartered Accountants

C. Olaf Boyce   1942–1947
Examiner of Companies,
Department of Insurance, Government of Canada

Robert L. Boynton   1942–1951
Controller, Honeywell Controls Limited

F. J. Bradley   1951–1957
Financial Analyst, Massey-Ferguson Ltd.

M. A. Bradshaw   1920–1926, 1929–1930
Retired

D. L. Brandell   1956–1963
Treasurer, Canadian Conifer Limited

Edward A. Braund   1958–1961
Accountant, Robinson Industrial-Crafts Limited

Thomas Brazier   1950–1954
Senior Financial Representative
Ontario Hospital Services Commission

John F. Broadhead   1946–1947
Partner, Eddis & Associates, Chartered Accountants

Walter P. Brock   1950–1959
Partner, Muirhead, Brock and Hudson, Chartered Accountants

R. S. Brookfield   1955–1961
Controller, Formex Company of Canada

Yvon R. Brosseau   1955–1959
Associé, Brosseau, Laroche & Cie, Comptables Agréés

J. Harold Broughton   1932–1946
Secretary-Treasurer
The Ontario Cancer Treatment and Research Foundation

John W. E. Brown   1948–1956
Vice-President and Comptroller, Pepsi-Cola Canada Ltd.

Kenneth G. Brown   1945–1952
Plant Accountant, Campbell Soup Company Ltd.

Vernon A. Brown   1950–1955
Comptroller, Office Specialty Limited

W. C. Browning 1921–1932
Comptroller of Accounts,
Treasury Department, Province of Ontario

R. G. Brownridge 1946–1957
Assistant Treasurer,
Canada and Dominion Sugar Company Limited

Léo Brunelle 1958–1961
Adjoint au Trésorier,
Commission des Ecoles Catholiques de Montréal

E. R. Brunsdon 1956–1961
Chief Internal Auditor,
National Drug and Chemical Company of Canada Limited

S. L. Richard Brunton 1961–1964
—

Arthur Bernard Buckworth 1905–1940
Retired

Abigail M. Burch 1918–1958
Retired

Frederick J. Burgess 1951–1958
In practice with
Price, Waterhouse & Co., Chartered Accountants

W. G. Burgess 1953–1961
Comptroller, Kirkland & Rose Ltd.

J. B. Burke 1954–1957
In practice, J. B. Burke, Chartered Accountant

M. Carleton Burnes 1939–1950
Treasurer, British Newfoundland Corporation Limited

R. Arrell Burnes 1935–1948
Secretary-Treasurer, Galt Brass Company Limited

T. F. Burton 1936–1943
General Manager, Bristol Cadmium Plating Co. Ltd.

James C. Butler 1957–1964
Treasurer, Town of Dollard des Ormeaux

J. W. Ross Caldwell 1949–1952
General Research, Supertest Petroleum Corp. Ltd.

Fred Callaway   1956–1963
Chief Accountant, Managers, Limited

William A. Calvert   1954–1960
Account Executive, Young & Rubicam Ltd.

A. Earle Cameron   1930–1936
Vice-President, Cane Associates Ltd.

Jay S. Cameron   1946–1954
Executive Vice-President & General Manager,
The Pedlar People Limited

R. S. Cameron   1957–1964
Midland-Osler Securities Limited

R. W. Cameron   1953–1963
Chief Accountant, H. M. Trimble & Sons Ltd.

Alexander Campbell   1939–1946
President, Gordon Hotels Ltd.

E. Douglas Campbell   1928–1937
President, Associates Investment Company

John Douglas Campbell   1935–1939
Executive Director of Alberta Hospital Plan,
Department of Public Health, Province of Alberta

L. J. H. Campbell   1941–1951
Controller of Finance,
Board of Education for the Township of North York

Reginald Campbell   1932–1941
Executive Vice-President, Falconbridge Nickel Mines Limited

R. G. Capel   1951–1956
Board of Education, Owen Sound

F. K. Carlisle   1931–1937
President, Playfair & Co. Limited

Gary L. Carlson   1953–1957
Manager, Rambler (Saskatoon) Ltd.

W. M. Carlyle   1948–1950
Partner, F. H. Black & Co., Chartered Accountants

Gordon H. Carney   1960–1964
In practice with Beaton, Mathieson & Co., Chartered Accountants

William P. Carr   1933–1945
Vice-President, A. C. Leslie & Co. Limited

John D. Carrie   1953–1959
*In practice with
Thorne, Mulholland, Howson & McPherson,
Chartered Accountants*

F. G. Carrotte   1957–1960
Plant Manager, Jamar Plywood Limited

David E. Carse   1962–1964
Chief Accountant, Allen-Bradley Canada Limited

G. W. J. Carter   1959–1963
Executive, Bowell McLean Motor Co. Ltd.

M. E. H. Carter   1949–1954
*Principal Finance Officer,
Medical Services, Department of National Health & Welfare*

William E. Case   1936–1947
Vice-President, Finance, W. J. Gage Limited

Charles L. E. Cathro   1948–1955
In practice with Price, Waterhouse & Co., Chartered Accountants

R. Catterson   1951–1953
Treasurer, Rapid Blue Print Ltd.

Willson Ross Catto   1929–1935
Credit Manager, Eastern Canada Stevedoring (1963) Ltd.

John L. Chadwick   1945–1950
Treasurer, Goebel Brewing Company

V. Howard Chadwick   1939–1948
Partner, Chadwick, Potts & Co., Chartered Accountants

Dixon S. Chant   1936–1944
Administrative Vice-President, Duplate Canada Limited

Jack Chesson   1952–1954
Chief Accountant, Royalite Oil Company Limited

Lane R. Chester   1926–1933
President, Maher Shoes Limited

Claude N. Clark   1949–1958
Chief Accountant, A. Morgan Maree Jr. & Associates

Philip T. Clark   1920–1930
In practice, Philip T. Clark, Chartered Accountant

C. B. Clarkson   1945–1950
Office Manager, Jacroy Canada Ltd.

Guy C. Clarkson   1946
Director of Economic Research, The Canadian Medical Association

J. R. Clarkson   1934–1939
President, Ruff Clarkson Steel Ltd.

R. C. Clarkson   1928–1939
Purchasing Agent, Kayson Plastic & Chemicals Ltd.

Arthur T. Coates   1945–1951
Secretary-Treasurer, R. Laidlaw Lumber Co. Limited

Blake A. Cockburn   1927–1933
Assistant-Comptroller, Simpsons-Sears Limited

Douglas A. Cole   1948–1955
General Auditor, Canadian Pittsburgh Industries Ltd.

Paul Collin   1948–1954
Cotiseur aux appels, Ministère du Revenu National

J. H. Collins   1926–1934
Comptroller, Liquor Control Board of Ontario

B. E. Colnett   1949–1961
*Assistant Manager,
Guardian-Union Group of Insurance Companies*

George Colvin   1943–1952
McCarthy & McCarthy, Barristers and Solicitors

Philip F. Connell   1946–1957
Comptroller, Canadian Westinghouse Company Limited

Geoffrey R. Conway   1956–1962
Research Officer, Royal Commission on Taxation

J. A. Conway   1953–1954
Vice-President and Controller, Pacific Finance Corporation

B. H. Cook   1943–1951
—

A. W. Coome 1938–1946
Controller, Falconbridge Nickel Mines Ltd.

André Corbeil 1960–1963
Secrétaire, Lallemand Inc.

Gary H. Corlett 1955–1961
Manager, Mine Accounting, Noranda Mines, Limited

André H. Corneille 1947–1953
Treasurer, Joseph Elie Ltd.

Gaston Courchesne 1957–1958
Service Provincial de l'Impôt sur le Revenu, Québec

W. Barry Coutts 1941–1956
Professor, School of Business, University of Toronto

R. A. Couture 1951–1952
Vérificateur interne senior, Hydro-Québec

P. Robert Cowan 1946–1951
*Manager, Administration,
Crown Zellerbach Building Materials Ltd.*

Louis W. Cowley 1923–1950
Treasurer, Burns Bros. and Denton Limited

Kenneth R. Craig 1949–1960
Comptroller, Arco Automatic Retail Co. Limited

Robert H. Crandall 1952–1959
Bursar, Queen's University

Harold E. Crate 1920–1926
*Partner,
Thorne, Mulholland, Howson & McPherson, Chartered Accountants*

J. Stuart Crawford 1914–1916, 1919–1922
Retired

R. Crawley 1958–1961
Student, Mathematics, Physics & Chemistry, University of Toronto

Lawrence W. Crocker 1952–1956
Accounting Co-ordinator, United Co-operatives

William Crompton 1942–1947
Comptroller, Silknit Limited

John J. Cronin 1952–1963
Controller, Holmes Foundry Limited

Allen L. Crummer 1960–1962
Comptroller, Klassen Homes Ltd.

Leonard S. Cummings 1952–1956
Secretary-Treasurer, Toronto Type Foundry Limited

Rufus A. Curry 1954–1957
Division Accountant,
Canadian Oil Division, Shell Canada Ltd.

J. K. Curzon 1941–1950
Assistant Treasurer & Office Manager,
Scott Misener Steamships Limited

G. L. Dakin 1948–1956
Assistant Treasurer, Canadian Delhi Oil Ltd.

Garnet Davey 1953–1963
National Leased Assets Limited

Raymond David 1956–1959
Vice-président exécutif, Corporation d'Expansion Financière

John C. Davies 1956–1961
Comptroller, Oxford Leaseholds Ltd.

W. E. Davies 1956–1960
Partner, Davies, Grant & Co., Chartered Accountants

Frank L. Day 1946–1948
Secretary-Treasurer,
Albertawest Forest Products Corporation Ltd.

Allan E. Deegan 1958–1963
Internal Auditor, Canadian National Railways

F. L. DeGuerre 1939–1951
Controller, James Lovick Limited

Daniel de Leeuw 1959–1962
Vérificateur interne, Canadien National

René Derome 1960–1961
En pratique avec
Raymond, Chabot, Martin, Paré & Cie, Comptables Agréés

K. J. Detlor 1953–1960
Supervisor, Sales Department Avon Products Limited

Douglas W. Deuchars 1963–1964
Accountant, Appleford Paper Products Limited

Joseph A. DiGiovanni 1958–1962
Treasurer, Creaghan & Archibald Limited

H. I. H. Dietz 1929–1937
*Secretary-Treasurer and a Director,
Kerr Steamships Limited*

Keith M. Dinsmore 1944–1947
Controller, Victoria University

Yvon Dionne 1958–1961
Associé, Dionne, Richard & Cie, Comptables Agréés

A. Denys M. Dobbie 1960–1961
*In practice with
Peat, Marwick, Mitchell & Co., Chartered Accountants*

J. P. Dolan 1956–1959
In practice, J. P. Dolan, Chartered Accountant

Albert R. Donnelly 1947–1950
Partner, Donnelly & MacKillican, Chartered Accountants

J. Bruce Douglas 1959–1962
Budget Officer, Reckitt & Colman (Canada) Limited

W. Blair Douglas 1951–1958
Assistant to the Comptroller, John Inglis Co. Limited

H. R. Dow 1936–1947
Secretary-Treasurer, Murray Printing & Gravure Limited

S. T. Down 1944–1950
Excise Tax Auditor, Department of National Revenue

Roger Drapeau 1957–1960
*Comptable-vérificateur,
Commission des Valeurs Mobilières du Québec*

E. T. Draper 1948–1955
Secretary-Treasurer, Pye Electronics Limited

J. R. Ducharme 1959–1964
Controller, Universal Signs Ltd.

R. W. Duckworth 1955–1960
Secretary-Treasurer, ASP Productions Limited

Paul J. Duggan 1946–1955
Comptroller, Canada Building Materials Limited

Robert S. Dunlop 1912–1917
Retired

W. Dunne 1946–1950
Secretary-Treasurer, S. McCord & Co. Limited

David F. Durnan 1954–1960
Comptroller, Encylopaedia Britannica of Canada, Ltd.

Harry C. Dwyer 1925–1934, 1939–1946
Imperial Metal & Wood Industries Ltd.

Thomas Michael Dyer 1960–1964
Accountant, Georgian Towers Hotel

W. A. Easton 1959–1964
Chief Accountant, Imco Container (Canada) Ltd.

Edward L. Edwards 1949–1962
Comptroller, Barrigan Woodwares Limited

G. B. Eisenberg 1958–1963
Consultant, Wm. Eisenberg & Co., Chartered Accountants

Charles R. Elliott 1928–1936
President, Conwest Exploration Company Limited

Norman F. Ellison 1937–1949
Chief Audit Accountant,
Provincial Auditor's Office, Government of Ontario

R. H. Ellison 1939–1956
Executive Vice-President, Canadian Collieries Resources Limited

G. P. A. Elmslie 1937–1949
Secretary-Treasurer, Bennett & Collins Limited

Harry D. Elmslie 1955–1956 1957–1961
Student, Waterloo Lutheran University

Roger M. J. Emery   1958–1963
President, Tilbest Foods Limited

Roger R. Emery   1956–1960
Theology Student, St. Peter's Seminary

John James English   1919–1936
Secretary-Treasurer, Woodlands Investments, Limited

W. J. Evans   1955–1962
Office Manager, The Master Builders Company, Ltd.

Charles H. Ewing   1943–1945
In practice, Charles H. Ewing, Chartered Accountant

W. G. Fenny   1928–1935
Financial Analyst, Department of Lands and Forests

Marsden D. Fenwick   1955–1962
*Secretary-Treasurer,
McKeag, Harris Realty & Development Co. Ltd.*

R. C. Ferguson   1953–1959
Controller, Canadian Laboratory Supplies Limited

S. C. Ferguson   1922–1942
In practice, S. C. Ferguson, Chartered Accountant

S. E. Field   1959–1963
Comptroller, Crane Supply Division of Crane Canada Limited

Ronald F. Findlay   1956–1961
Chief Accountant, Canadian Schenley Ltd.

A. H. Fisher   1948–1958
Member of Council, Metropolitan Corporation of Greater Winnipeg

Eric N. Fisher   1949–1954
Controller, Northern Stores (Eastern), Hudson's Bay Company

John H. Fisher   1950–1956
Secretary-Treasurer, J. D. Crighton International Ltd.

K. Maxwell Fleming   1957–1963
Assistant Comptroller, Eastern Canada Stevedoring (1963) Ltd.

Paul Edwin Fleming   1944–1950
In practice, Paul Edwin Fleming, Chartered Accountant

Wilfrid B. Flynn 1942–1946
Assessor, Taxation Division, Department of National Revenue

J. E. Forden 1959–1964
Canadian Industries Limited

Georges Fortin 1949–1953
Comptable en chef, La Banque Provinciale du Canada

George Foster 1943–1953
President, Associated Printers Limited

J. C. Fowler 1946–1954
Partner, Touche, Ross, Bailey & Smart, Chartered Accountants

Charles A. Frank 1946–1950
Accountant, York University

Charles Clifford Frankiss 1960–1961
Assistant to Partner,
Hancock, Gilbert & Morris, Chartered Accountants

J. Ramsey Fraser 1934–1936
Executive Vice-President, A. W. Homme Ltd.

A. P. Friesen 1946–1947
Vice-President, Secretary and Treasurer,
The White Pass & Yukon Corporation Limited

Ralph Froment 1956–1962
Partner,
McClary, George, Cordingley & Froment, Chartered Accountants

A. J. Frost 1930–1931
Assistant General Manager, Guaranty Trust Co. of Canada

Gordon I. Froud 1948–1956
Treasurer,
Nacionale Manufacturera de Cauchos y Neumaticos General

Loyd H. Fryer 1961–1963
Partner, A. F. Gosling & Co., Chartered Accountants

Georges R. Gagnon 1952–1955
Directeur adjoint, Vente Marchandise,
Secteur de Montréal, Canadien National

J. M. Gagnon 1957–1959
Professeur, Faculté de Commerce, Université Laval

J. J. Garwood 1957–1961
Assistant Controller, Telegram Publishing Co. Limited

J. N. Geddes 1959–1964
Divisional Controller,
Minnesota Mining & Manufacturing of Canada Ltd.

R. N. Gell 1958–1961
Gell Travel Bureau and The Treasure Shop

N. B. Gerry 1916–1927
Retired

Arnold T. Gibb 1941–1955
Audit Manager, C.I.T. Financial Corporation

Gordon Gibson 1950–1960
Account Executive, Merrill, Lynch, Pierce, Fenner & Smith Inc.

Hume Gibson 1926–1934
Vice-President & Manager, John Wood Company Limited

Gordon B. Gill 1950–1955
Manager,
Thorne, Mulholland, Howson & McPherson, Chartered Accountants

W. B. Girdwood 1960–1964
Chief Accountant, Ontario Branch Stores, T. Eaton Co. Ltd.

Gordon A. Gislason 1942–1952
Partner, G. A. Gislason & Co., Chartered Accountants

C. V. Gladwell 1941–1944
Supervisor,
Touche, Ross, Bailey & Smart, Chartered Accountants

J. Grant Glassco 1931–1957
President,
Brazilian Traction, Light and Power Company, Limited

J. Douglas Goforth 1949–1952
Treasurer & Controller, Lenkurt Electric Co. of Canada, Ltd.

Hon. Walter L. Gordon 1927–1963
Minister of Finance, Government of Canada

D. Russell Gormley 1939–1948
Vice-President, Consumers Glass Company Limited

Bruce D. Gowdy 1954–1958
Comptroller, Perini Land & Development Co.

Barry M. Graham 1954–1960
North Western Securities Ltd.

John Graham 1957–1960
Supervisor, Accounting, Confederation Life Association

Kenneth O. Grant 1955–1960
Chief Accountant, Federal-Mogul-Bower (Canada) Ltd.

Malcolm E. Grant 1956–1960
Partner, Davies, Grant & Co., Chartered Accountants

Ivan S. Gray 1922–1932
Partner, Gray, Butcher, Frost, Smith, Chartered Accountants

Bremner B. Green 1948–1955
Executive Assistant to President, Bowes Co. Ltd.

Edward W. H. Green 1949–1955
Secretary-Treasurer, Air Terminal Transport

Harold A. Green 1946–1956
Controller, Cole Steel International Ltd.

J. D. Green 1931–1937
Export Manager and Vice-President, Hiram Walker & Sons Limited

C. G. Greenfield 1943–1946
Director, Moss Lawson & Co. Ltd.

J. Esmond Grier 1925–1927
Partner, Grier, Dyer & Co., Chartered Accountants

William Griffin 1953–1961
Administrative Assistant to Superintendent, University of Toronto

Frederick Grossman 1956–1963
Income Tax Assessor, Department of National Revenue

Gordon E. Grundy 1931–1936
*President, Automotive Division,
Studebaker Corporation, Studebaker of Canada Limited*

R. A. Hall 1953–1959
Assistant Treasurer, Molson Breweries Limited

William C. Hall 1956–1960
In practice with
Monteith, Riehl, Waters & Co., Chartered Accountants

A. S. Hallamore 1944–1945
President, A. S. Hallamore & Associates Ltd.

A. R. Hamilton 1952–1955, 1959–1960
Controller, Dominion Building Materials Ltd.

B. Myles Hamilton 1956–1959
Executive Assistant, General Bakeries Limited

E. A. Hamilton 1947–1952
Comptroller, Brewers Warehousing Co. Limited

L. L. B. Hamlin 1941–1964
Secretary-Treasurer, Canadian Order of Foresters

T. J. Hammett 1929–1936
Partner, Cox & Hammett, Chartered Accountants

T. M. Hanlon 1956–1959
Partner, Burroughs, Hanlon & Weber, Chartered Accountants

J. R. Hanna 1959–1963
Student,
Graduate School of Business Administration, University of Michigan

H. S. Hanson 1948–1953
Retired

V. D. Harbinson 1913–1919
Partner, V. D. Harbinson & Co., Chartered Accountants

E. M. Harbour 1929–1941
Chief Accountant,
Connaught Medical Research Laboratories, University of Toronto

Peter T. Harrington 1953–1957
Refinery Manufacturing Coordinator, Mobil Oil Company
de Venezuela

Walter P. Harrower, 1957–1963
Canadian International Paper Company

G. William Hawes 1937–1944
Comptroller, Maple Leaf Mills Limited

Gordon H. Hawkett 1956–1964
Canadian Corporate Management Co. Limited

M. M. Hawkrigg 1952–1959
General Manager, Fuller Brush Company, Limited

Charles W. Hay 1949–1950
In practice, Charles W. Hay, Chartered Accountant

Harold E. Hayes 1956–1959
Division Chief, Auditor General of Canada

Harrison C. Hayes 1926–1927
Partner, McDonald, Currie & Co., Chartered Accountants

John R. Hayes 1951–1957
Assistant Secretary-Treasurer,
The Winnipeg School Division No. 1

P. G. Healey 1948–1950
National Sales Supervisor, London Free Press Printing Co. Ltd.

H. Rodney Heard 1937–1948
Secretary, Mid-North Engineering Services Limited

R. H. B. Hector 1926–1930
Partner, Cossar, Hector, Payne & Co., Chartered Accountants

J. P. Hemmant 1952–1954
Comptroller, S. Smith & Sons (Canada) Ltd.

J. A. B. Henderson 1932–1934
Metropolitan Toronto Audit Department

R. M. Henderson 1946–1951
Comptroller, Hilton Hotels (U.K.) Ltd.

Roy D. Henderson 1945–1947
Assistant Manager, Kingcome Navigation Co. Ltd.

J. S. Hendrie 1945–1948
Teacher, Hamilton Board of Education

Norman A. Henry 1942–1956
Secretary-Treasurer, Newman Steel Warehouse Ltd.

J. D. Hickman 1947–1953
Works Accountant, Heavy Organic Chemicals Division, I.C.I. Ltd.

Barry E. Hicks   1956–1961
Assistant Director of Extension for Professional Courses,
McMaster University

A. C. Hill   1927–1934
Vice-President & General Manager, Wilkinson and Kompass Limited

C. J. Hill   1948–1952
Managing Director, Mitchell Insurance Agencies Ltd.

R. Douglas Hill   1913–1922
Retired

A. G. Holman   1939–1942
Comptroller, Diesel Equipment Ltd.

Hartley R. Holmes   1930–1936
Partner, Deloitte, Plender, Haskins & Sells, Chartered Accountants

Kenneth R. Holmquist   1957–1964
Supervisor, Special Projects,
United Community Fund of Greater Toronto

C. E. Hook   1960–1964
Office Manager, Barber Tractor and Parts Ltd.

James V. Hooper   1948–1951
Director & Treasurer, Gairdner & Company Limited

Henry A. Hopkins   1918–1928
Retired

Gordon W. Horne   1951–1955
Partner, Waters, Savage, Horne & Ronson, Chartered Accountants

B. MacLean Howard   1957–1963
Manager, Budgets & Analysis,
Philco Corporation of Canada Limited

Vernon W. Howe   1950–1962
Treasurer, Versafood Services Limited

Gordon E. Howey   1955–1959
Accountant, McNamara Corporation Limited

Richard V. Howson   1951–1956
Assistant to Vice-President,
Finance and Administration, Levy Industries Limited

R. E. Hubling   1953–1959
Assistant Secretary-Treasurer, Canadian Steelcase Company Limited

G. O. Huggan 1935–1947
Secretary-Treasurer & Comptroller,
Supreme Aluminum Industries Limited

Stanley E. Hulbert 1955–1960
Chief Accountant, Toronto General Hospital

S. H. Humphrys 1944–1952
Treasurer, International Water Supply Ltd.

D. G. A. Hunt 1953–1960
Sihi Pumps Limited

Thomas L. Hurdman 1955–1959
Comptroller, Montreal Branch, The Royal Trust Company

P. M. Hutcheson 1938–1942
Assessor, Taxation Division, Department of National Revenue

John L. Hutchings 1949–1952
Assistant Secretary & Controller,
Flint Engineering & Construction Ltd.

W. Farrell Hyde 1954–1955
Partner, Hyde, Houghton & Co., Chartered Accountants

Robert W. Inglis 1946–1955
Secretary, Scudder International Investments Ltd.

F. M. Innes 1959–1964
Assessor, Income Tax Division, Department of National Revenue

Michael Ireland 1951–1957
Assessor, Taxation Division, Department of National Revenue

G. E. Irvine 1946–1953
Manager, Manufacturing Division, Thompson Products Limited

Douglas D. W. Irwin 1938–1942
Partner,
Winspear, Higgins, Stevenson & Doane, Chartered Accountants

Allan G. Isbister 1939–1953
Secretary and Treasurer, The Jockey Club Limited

R. D. Isbister 1937–1950
Vice-President, Duncan Lithographing Company Ltd.

Charles W. I. Jackson 1929–1938
Vice-President and Treasurer, Coca Cola Ltd.

Raymond R. Jackson   1949–1961
Manager, Overseas Financial Controls, RCA International Division

Norman H. W. James   1954–1961
Accounting Department Manager, United Co-operatives of Ontario

J. M. Jamieson   1926–1954
Manager of Plant Accounting,
Hydro-Electric Power Commission of Ontario

J. D. Jarvis   1945–1950
Comptroller, The Dumont Aluminum Limited

Walter J. Jennings   1946–1954
Treasurer, General Steel Wares Limited

R. G. Johnson   1959–1960
Partner, Turnbull & Johnson, Chartered Accountants

D. Ross Johnston   1955–1958
In practice, D. Ross Johnston, Chartered Accountant

Harry Johnston   1938–1946
Internal Auditor, General Steel Wares Limited

John Johnston   1954–1963
Assistant Controller,
Mack Trucks Manufacturing Company of Canada Ltd.

Alan C. Johnstone   1951–1957
Minister (Assistant to Presiding Bishop),
The Reorganized Church of Jesus Christ of Latter Day Saints

W. Kenneth Jones   1947–1952
Controller, Central Region, T. Eaton Co. Ltd.

Lawson A. Kaake   1941–1953
Vice-President and General Manager, Upper Lakes Shipping Ltd.

W. M. Karney   1950–1954
Financial Examiner, National Energy Board

E. K. Karvonen   1958–1962
Controller, Cornelius Manufacturing Co. Ltd.

Derek G. Keaveney   1947–1955
Controller, Canadian Imperial Bank of Commerce

P. J. Keenan   1954–1956
Assistant Treasurer & Comptroller, Patino Mining Corporation

John M. Kennaley 1956–1962
Secretary-Treasurer, The Richards Glass Co. Limited

A. A. Kennedy 1954–1961
Secretary and Treasurer, Collins & Aikman Limited

A. M. Kennedy 1952–1960
Assistant Comptroller, Gazette Printing Company Limited

Miles Kennedy 1952–1955
Associate Professor of Industrial Management,
Massachusetts Institute of Technology

A. H. Kerr 1952–1954
Assistant Comptroller & Chief Accountant,
Canada Trust—Huron & Erie

Robert C. Kilgour 1941–1946
Partner, V. D. Harbinson & Co., Chartered Accountants

K. D. Kimmerly 1952–1959
Division Controller, Sheller Manufacturing Corporation

P. G. Kingsburgh 1922–1943
Retired

J. G. Kingsmill 1938–1950
In practice, J. G. Kingsmill, Management Consultant

G. D. K. Kinnaird 1956–1958
Retired

Roger M. Kirkpatrick 1951–1955
Head of Geography Department, Trinity College Schools

Tom M. Kirkwood 1941–1949
Vice-President and General Manager, La Brasserie Labatt Limitée

Walter H. Kitto 1950
Partner,
Meredith, Bruce, Baldwin & Kitto, Chartered Accountants

R. C. Kjeldson 1949–1956
Co-ordinator for Transportation & Supply, Imperial Oil Ltd.

Daniel E. Knechtel 1955–1960
Assistant to Controller, T. Eaton Co. Ltd.

William G. Konantz 1945–1951
President, North American Lumber and Supply Company (Limited)

W. W. Kramer 1953–1958
Secretary-Treasurer, Dare Foods Limited

Arthur S. Labatt 1956–1962
Security Analyst, McLeod, Young, Weir & Co. Limited

John P. Labatt 1948–1950
Vice-President, Ontario Division, Labatt's Ontario Breweries Limited

Ray C. Lackenbauer 1962–1964
Assistant to Controller, Jamesway Co. Limited

Alan Laing 1947–1955
Assistant Comptroller, Dominion Foundries and Steel, Limited

W. D. Lake 1939–1952
In practice, W. D. Lake, Chartered Accountant

W. D. Land 1952–1953
Director, Simplicity Products Ltd.

J. S. Lang 1939–1943
Internal Auditor
British Columbia Hydro and Power Authority

L. L. G. Langford 1961–1963
In practice with Collins & Hames, Chartered Accountants

J. A. Langhorne 1950–1955
Partner,
Humpage, Taylor, McDonald & Co., Chartered Accountants

Thomas W. Langstone 1924–1934
Retired

B. E. Lanning 1956–1961
Controller, American-Standard Products (Canada) Limited

R. T. LaPrairie 1949–1955
Comptroller, The Royal Trust Company

A. A. Lavallee 1951–1955
Vice-President, Finance, Eddy Match Company, Limited

Alan M. Lavine 1959–1962
Manager, Pape, Strom, Sherman & Lavine, Chartered Accountants

J. A. Lavoie 1948–1950
Ministère de la Santé,
Services de l'Assurance Hospitalisation, Québec

F. Alan Lawson 1950–1955
President, Consolidated Factors Corp. Ltd.

F. R. L. Lazier 1940–1942
Assistant-Treasurer, Black, Clawson-Kennedy Ltd.

Geo. F. Leaver 1917–1946
President, The Canadian Wool Company Limited

D. A. LeBaron 1950–1951, 1953–1954
Senior Auditor, DuPont of Canada Ltd.

R. Bruce Ledingham 1956–1959
Partner,
Munn, Richards, Yeoman & Co., Chartered Accountants

W. Lee 1954–1958
—

A. H. Lenec 1954
Partner, Lenec & Le Gallais, Chartered Accountants

Norman R. A. Leschak 1957–1962
Chief Accountant & Assistant Secretary-Treasurer,
The Trustees of the Toronto General Burying Grounds

Kenneth M. Leslie 1950–1954, 1962–1963
Executive Director,
Hamilton & District Association for Retarded Children

O. T. L'Esperance 1929–1933, 1941–1946
Treasurer, Empire Silversmiths Limited

Kenneth F. Lewis 1959–1964
Kerr Addison Mines Limited

M. E. Lewis 1958–1963
Secretary, Hodge Industrial Securities Limited

J. H. Lindsey 1916–1943
Brazilian Traction, Light and Power Company, Limited

D. R. Linney 1954–1960
Financial Analyst, Shell Canada Limited

James H. Lippert 1953–1961
Controller, Laura Secord Candy Shops Limited

John Lonergan 1951–1956
Comptroller, Dietrich-Collins Equipment Ltd.

F. Lorenzen   1927–1935
Partner, Lorenzen & Lesonsky, Chartered Accountants

Gaëtan Losier   1957–1959
Contrôleur, Geo. Demers, Ing.-Conseil

T. Ralph Lougheed   1960–1963
Research Department, Wood Gundy & Co. Ltd.

W. L. Louth   1952–1962
Comptroller, Toronto General Hospital

Donovan R. Lytle   1955–1956
Assistant Treasurer, Atlantic Acceptance Corporation Limited

Hudson M. Lytle   1952–1960
Comptroller, E. H. Price, Limited

B. L. MacAlpine   1952–1955
Vice-President & Secretary-Treasurer,
Imperial Furniture Manufacturing Co. Limited

Bain Macaskill   1949–1952
Comptroller, Molson's Brewery (Ontario) Limited

Arthur R. MacCallum   1934–1941
President, American-Standard Products (Canada) Limited

A. L. MacDonald   1951–1955
Partner,
Wright, Erickson, Lee & MacDonald, Chartered Accountants

John C. MacEachen   1959–1963
Chief Accountant, Thor Mills Limited

Donald Allen Macfarlane   1945–1955
Treasurer, Rio Algom Mines Limited

D. A. MacFarlane   1945–1952
Assistant Secretary-Treasurer, St. Mary's Cement Co., Limited

John A. MacFarlane   1958–1962
Chief Accountant, University of Western Ontario

G. Ralph MacGougan   1951–1959
Department of Defence Production, Comptroller's Branch

Bruce S. MacGowan   1955–1962
Assistant Secretary-Treasurer, Fry & Company Limited

W. A. Macintosh 1957–1961
Retired

J. R. M. Mackay 1959–1963
Teacher, North York Board of Education

James A. MacKillican 1948–1953
Partner, Donnelly & MacKillican, Chartered Accountants

Ian M. Mackinnon 1948–1958
Secretary-Treasurer, H. Corby Distillery Limited

Ian G. A. MacMillan 1949–1958
Controller, Mack Trucks Manufacturing Company of Canada Ltd.

Donald M. MacPherson 1957–1962
Manager, Data Processing, Greenshields Inc.

W. D. MacVicar 1949–1957
Controller, Clevite Limited

Morley K. Maddock 1958–1963
Executive Office Accountant, Campbell Chibougamau Mines Ltd.

A. J. Maes 1954–1960
Comptroller, Douglas Hunter Limited

J. Lawrence Magee 1950–1954
Partner, J. L. Magee & Associates, Accountants

Michael M. Maguire 1952–1960
Secretary-Treasurer, Bowring Brothers Ltd.

W. B. Malone 1922–1935
*Vice-President & Financial Consultant to the President,
Rio Algom Mines Limited*

W. P. E. Mang 1954–1960
Controller, Hectors Ltd.

Alan R. Marchment 1950–1955
Président Directeur Général, Transamerica International S.A.

Guy Marinier 1952–1954
Trésorier, Les Distilleries Melchers Ltée

Howard K. Marks 1959–1962
Investment Analyst, Confederation Life Association

S. C. Marks 1950–1954
Manager, Harris, Kerr, Forster & Company

J. F. Marshall 1961–1964
Assistant Comptroller, Eastern & Chartered Trust Company

E. D. K. Martin 1939–1951
Chief Tax Accountant, Imperial Oil Limited

James R. Martin 1948–1953
Comptroller, Gilvesy Construction Ltd.

Joseph P. Martin 1955–1960
Secretary, Raymond's Nut Shops Ltd.

S. C. H. Martin 1924–1943
Proprietor, Martin Counselling Service

Victor Mathurin 1957–1964
Supervisor,
Bernstein, Bernstein, Wile & Gordon, Certified Public Accountants

Wilmot L. Matthews 1958–1961
Analyst, Fry & Company Limited

Lawrence S. Mattson 1954–1958
Internal Auditor, Sunbeam Corporation (Canada) Ltd.

D. J. Maybee 1952–1959
Research Secretary, The Hospital for Sick Children

Charles L. McAlpine 1956–1959
Secretary, Campbell Chibougamau Mines Ltd.

W. Eric McBain 1918–1923
—

Charles J. McCabe 1925–1932
In practice, Charles J. McCabe, Chartered Accountant

John E. McCamus 1947–1952
Director of Finance, Prairie Division, John Labatt Limited

B. K. McCandless 1953–1958
Accountant, Pemberton Realty Corporation Limited

Clifford McCarten 1949–1954
Treasurer, Croven Ltd.

John P. McCarter 1952–1958
General Accounting Manager, Massey-Ferguson Limited

Andrew G. McCaughey 1949–1953
Secretary-Treasurer, Canadian Marconi Company

Douglas J. McClellan 1931–1947
Comptroller of Revenue
Treasury Department, Government of Province of Ontario

William A. McColl 1953–1959
Assistant Controller, Hudson's Bay Company

William B. McDiarmid 1952–1960
Financial Analyst, Miron Company Ltd.

Daniel L. McDonald 1956–1959
Assistant Professor, University of British Columbia

F. Beattie McDonald 1953–1957
Secretary-Treasurer, Stanton Pipes (Canada) Limited

W. Jack McDougall 1937–1941
Professor,
School of Business Administration, University of Western Ontario

Desmond H. McElney 1957–1961
Ranco Controls S.p.A.

Robert L. McFarlane 1940–1941
Seabridge Investments Ltd.

John A. McGeachie 1949–1955
Secretary-Treasurer, Custom-Aire Aluminum Limited

Maurice Gerrard McGinley 1958–1961
Deputy Secretary-Treasurer, Edmonton Public School Board

Arthur Robert McGinn 1920–1941
Secretary and Treasurer and Director,
Anaconda American Brass Limited

Robert L. McGuire 1953–1958
Assessor, Taxation Division, Department of National Revenue

W. N. McKay 1960–1964
In practice, W. N. McKay, Chartered Accountant

James A. McKee 1944–1958
Secretary-Treasurer, Canadian Corporate Management Co. Limited

John R. McKeeman 1950–1959
Assistant Treasurer, Falconbridge Nickel Mines Limited

Fred K. McKenzie 1948–1952
Secretary-Treasurer, Mohawk Handle Co. Ltd.

Warren R. McKeown 1951–1962
Secretary-Treasurer, Fry & Company Limited

James I. McKinney 1956–1961
Secretary-Treasurer, Hardifoam Products Limited

Arch. Hodge McLachlin 1920–1929
Retired

Walter McNally 1952–1958
Superintendent, Income Taxes, Northern Electric Co. Ltd.

Duncan V. McPherson 1952–1956
Manager, Price, Waterhouse & Co., Chartered Accountants

Isabel McPherson 1941–1955
Retired

A. R. McPhie 1945–1950
In practice, A. R. McPhie, Chartered Accountant

D. N. McPhie 1947–1951
Manager, Budget Administration,
Canadian Westinghouse Company Limited

J. T. McWhirter 1940–1945
Treasurer, Falconbridge Nickel Mines Limited

Donald S. Merson 1952–1964
Executive Assistant to the Controller,
Canadian Imperial Bank of Commerce

Ernest B. Meyers 1945–1950
Chief Internal Auditor, Canadian National Railways

L. Murray Michols 1945–1958
Comptroller, Calgary Brewing and Malting Company Limited

John G. Midghall 1942–1953
Executive, Eastern Etching & Manufacturing Co.

H. H. Milburn 1929–1938
Director, Assessments Branch,
Taxation Division, Department of National Revenue

David F. Miller 1960–1962
In practice with
Arthur Young, Clarkson, Gordon & Co., Accountants & Auditors

John Miller 1951–1954
Manager, Tax Department, Union Carbide Canada Limited

R. G. Mills 1957–1962
Controller, Burro Gas & Electric Ltd.

Wiley J. Millyard 1936–1943
Canadian Consul & Trade Commissioner, Canadian Government

Frank W. Milne 1949–1955
Assistant to Management, Colombian Petroleum Company

Kenneth A. Miners 1930–1948
Vice-President & Treasurer, The Great Lakes Paper Company Limited

William P. Mitchell 1952–1956
Assistant Controller, Financial Analysis, Ford Motor Co. of Canada

John P. Moloney 1947–1953
Manager, Accounting Services,
American-Standard Products (Canada) Limited

Hon. J. Waldo Monteith 1930–1933
Member of the Parliament of Canada,
Partner,
Monteith, Monteith & Company, Chartered Accountants

John H. Moore 1937–1953
President, John Labatt Limited

W. L. Moran 1938–1947
Secretary-Treasurer, Equipment Sales and Services Limited

D. Norman Morris 1953–1958
Treasurer and Controller, Joy Manufacturing Company (Canada) Ltd.

George W. Morrison 1957–1962
Internal Auditor, Canadian National Railways

K. J. Morrison 1960–1963
Retired

Thomas A. Movold 1952–1959
Assistant Controller, Canada Barrels & Kegs Limited

John G. Muir 1956–1962
Assessor, Taxation Division, Department of National Revenue

Alex Muirhead 1954–1958
Partner, Muirhead, Brock & Hudson, Chartered Accountants

Gertrude Mulcahy 1943–1949
Research Associate,
Canadian Institute of Chartered Accountants

George H. Mundy 1948–1955
Comptroller, S. A. Armstrong Limited

D. H. Munger 1934–1939
Comptroller and Director,
International Harvester Co. (S.A.) (Pty.) Ltd.

G. A. Murless 1955–1961
Comptroller, Fengate Publishing Co. Ltd.

George J. Murphy 1953–1962
Professor, University of Saskatchewan

Gerald A. Murray 1950–1957
Director of Management Accounting,
Simpson, Riddell, Stead, & Partners, Management Consultants

D. T. Myers 1940–1950
Myers Brothers

M. J. Neal 1958–1963
Comptroller, Gillies Bros. & Co. Ltd.

R. R. Neale 1949–1955
Treasurer, Brennan Paving Co., Ltd.

W. K. Nelson 1946–1951
—

D. W. Newborn 1949–1952
Partner, Ross, Newborn & Co., Chartered Accountants

John F. Newton 1955–1958
Secretary-Treasurer, J. Diamond & Sons Ltd.

Lawrence M. Nichols 1952–1961
Comptroller, Baton Broadcasting Limited

S. R. Nicholson 1945–1953
Manager, Internal Audit Department, The Robert Simpson Co. Ltd.

K. E. Noble 1950–1954
Joint Interest Auditor, United Canso Oil & Gas Ltd.

Margaretta Norrish 1918–1950
Retired

Patrick Northey 1958–1963
Vice-President, Finance, Breithaupt, Milsom & Benson Ltd.

Fred L. Norwood 1946–1947
Treasurer, Supertest Petroleum Corp. Ltd.

J. A. O'Brian 1947–1952
Vice-President, Hendrie & Co. Ltd.

J. Robert O'Hara 1960–1963
Assistant Accountant, Bohemian Maid Brewing Company Limited

J. R. Ohrling 1960–1964
John Labatt Limited (Brewing Division)

J. W. Oldfield 1951–1955
Vice-President, Finance and Administration, Gordon Hotels Ltd.

Peter F. Oliphant 1953–1961
Senior Accountant, Shell Canada Limited

R. Ernest Oliver 1948–1951
Secretary-Treasurer, Donald Ropes & Wire Cloth Limited

Earl H. Orser 1950–1961
Vice-President and Treasurer, Anthes Imperial Limited

Michael Osborne 1951–1953
Treasurer, Talisman Mines Ltd.

Orville F. Osborne 1956–1961
Partner, Osborne & Osborne, Chartered Accountants

C. V. Outridge 1957–1961
Plant Accountant, Canada Iron Foundries, Limited

Donald C. Pace 1941–1952
Secretary-Treasurer, Amalgamated Electric Corp. Ltd.

Robert H. C. Page 1923–1928, 1941–1942
Controller, Aircraft Appliances & Equipment Ltd.

Fred R. Palin 1928–1936
*President and General Manager,
Union Gas Company of Canada, Limited*

J. A. Palmer 1955–1961
In practice with McDonald, Currie & Co., Chartered Accountants

Paul H. Palmer 1955–1962
Controller, York Steel Construction Limited

L. A. Paré 1955–1959
Comptroller, The Northern Life Assurance Co. of Canada

H. Bruce Parkes 1946–1956
*General Manager and Director,
Encyclopaedia Britannica of Canada, Ltd.*

Geoffrey R. Parsons 1957–1960
*In practice with
John R. Parsons & Company, Certified Public Accountants*

Nora M. Partridge 1941–1947
In practice, Nora M. Partridge, Chartered Accountant

G. S. Patchet 1945–1951
Controller, Delta Acceptance Corporation Limited

Norman A. Patterson 1952–1960
President, Patterson's Limited

William H. Patterson 1956–1961
Partner, Davies, Grant & Patterson, Chartered Accountants

Gregory B. Pattison 1925–1934
Office Manager, Gord Blanche Co. Ltd.

A. Edwin Payne 1941–1945
*Chief Accountant & Office Manager,
La France Textiles Canada Limited*

John E. Payne 1954–1960
Office Manager, The Central Pipe Line Co. Ltd.

Morgan C. Payne 1951–1956
Controller, Head Office, Anthes Imperial Limited

Westell G. Peaker 1953–1963
Anaconda American Brass Ltd.

Gaston Pelletier 1959–1963
*Professeur,
Ecole des Hautes Etudes Commerciales, Université de Montréal*

R. E. Pennington 1948–1954
Accountant & Office Manager,
London Printing & Lithographing Co. Limited

D. S. Perigoe 1935–1939
Vice-President and Managing Director,
Telegram Publishing Co. Limited

Douglas E. Perrin 1949–1957
Manager, Headquarters Accounting,
Canadian Westinghouse Company Limited

Rémi M. Petit 1957–1958
Contrôleur, Clinique Métropolitaine Ltée

W. P. Petrie 1954–1957
Treasurer, The Toronto Iron Works Limited

H. Pinnock 1919–1934
Noranda Mines, Limited

Herbert J. B. Pointer 1952–1957
Chief Accountant, Producers Pipelines Ltd.

. G. Howard Poland 1955–1961
Assistant to Comptroller, Coca-Cola Ltd.

J. D. Porter 1945–1957
Assistant General Manager, Canada Permanent Trust Company

Guy Poupart 1959–1964
Service de la Taxe de Vente, Québec

William W. Prest 1946–1951
Internal auditor, Atomic Energy of Canada Ltd.

Harold D. Pringle 1948–1952
Partner, Owen, Pringle & Co., Chartered Accountants

W. G. Pringle 1956–1960
Partner, Purdy, Giles, Wyllie, Pringle & Co., Chartered Accountants

Donald F. Prowse 1949–1953
Vice-President, Windfields Farm Limited

D. W. Ptolemy 1954–1962
Business Manager, Boy Scouts of Canada, Greater Toronto Region

F. C. Pugh 1941
Chief Accountant, Victoria and Grey Trust Company

Andrew Purdon   1929–1942
In practice, Andrew Purdon, Chartered Accountant

Russell H. Purdy   1944–1946
Partner, Purdy, Giles, Wyllie, Pringle & Co., Chartered Accountants

Frank C. Putt   1929–1936
Vice-President, Imperial Carpet Distributors Limited

F. D. Pynn   1953–1959
Manager Corporate Accounts, BP Canada Limited

Alan A. Querney   1954–1957
Secretary-Treasurer, Austin Lumber (Dalton) Limited

C. H. Quilliam   1960–1963
Partner, Quilliam & Stuart, Chartered Accountants

Ronald H. Raisman   1959–1962
Executive Assistant to the President and Chief Accountant,
CTV Television Network Ltd.

Alex G. Rankin   1938–1947
Vice-President, Finance, British Columbia Forest Products Ltd.

W. C. Rankin   1952–1959
Assistant to Vice-President, Finance, The Globe and Mail Limited

Duncan E. W. Rapier   1952–1955
Comptroller, Nassau Beach Hotel

J. H. Ratcliffe   1917–1918
Chairman of the Board, McLeod, Young, Weir & Co. Ltd.

John R. Rathwell   1956–1958
Partner, Ward, Watson & Rathwell, Chartered Accountants

W. T. Read   1952–1957
Retired

D. Ronald Reason   1954–1960
Accounting Manager,
Addressograph-Multigraph of Canada Ltd.

S. P. Reesor
In practice, Stuart P. Reesor, Chartered Accountant

J. S. Reeves   1924–1931
Director, Taxation, Department of National Revenue

T. Raymond Reid   1961–1962
Director and Secretary, Thomas Reid (Chemists) Ltd.

André J. Renaud 1954–1956
Chef comptable, Compagnie Miron Ltée

Oleg Revenko 1957–1963
Credit Officer, Industrial Development Bank

E. J. Reynolds 1950–1953
Treasurer, Saskatchewan Power Corporation

C. A. Rice 1949–1952
Partner, H. R. Doane & Company, Chartered Accountants

Earle B. Richards 1939–1949
Vice-President, Finance, The Globe and Mail Limited

George C. Richards 1952–1955
Controller, Eastern Chemical Division,
Hooker Chemical Corporation

John E. Richardson 1954–1963
Student,
Graduate School of Business Administration, Harvard University

John S. Richardson 1959–1964
Assistant Comptroller, John Labatt Limited

D. F. Ritchie 1953–1963
Secretary-Treasurer, F. W. Fearman Company, Limited

F. Neil Robarts 1958–1962
Internal Auditor, Anthes Imperial Limited

Roland B. Roberts 1950–1956
Assistant Treasurer, The Jockey Club Limited

James P. Robertson 1941–1948
Partner, Campbell, Lawless & Punchard, Chartered Accountants

C. Gordon Robinson 1935–1949
Executive Vice-President, Hanson Transport Co. Ltd.

E. Carey Robinson 1939–1951
Administrator, The St. Catharines General Hospital

H. I. Robinson 1937–1946
Accountant, Canadian Transport Tariff Bureau Association

Henry A. Robinson 1950–1955
Accountant, W. R. Brock Limited

Howard W. A. Robinson 1946–1949
Assessor, Department of National Revenue

R. A. Robinson 1948–1956
Comptroller, Western Decalta Petroleum Limited

W. G. M. Robinson 1935–1948
Comptroller, Pigott Construction Co. Ltd.

J. A. Robson 1926–1933
Comptroller and Treasurer, Jordan Wines Limited

Robert J. Rooks 1955–1958
In practice with
Tinkham, Wells & Co., Chartered Accountants

Joseph J. Rorai 1957–1961
Comptroller, Consumer Credit Corporation Limited

D. Douglas Ross 1934–1946
Senior Financial Analyst, International Latex Corp.

John C. Ross 1934–1940
Associate Manager-Secretary-Treasurer,
Canadian Co-operative Wool Growers Ltd.

Gordon S. Rowan 1951–1956, 1960–1961
Senior Internal Auditor, Canadian National Railways

Robert G. Rudolf 1924–1929
Retired

Jack E. Rupert 1945–1950
Chief Auditor,
Department of Attorney General, Province of Ontario

John C. Rutledge 1956–1962
Treasurer, Parker Brothers Games Ltd.

Norman C. Saint 1949–1962
Secretary and Treasurer, The Metropolitan Trust Company

R. G. Saunders 1945–1951, 1953–1955
Treasurer, United Keno Hill Mines Limited

William J. Saunderson 1956–1964
Nesbitt, Thomson and Company, Limited

H. A. Sawyer   1925–1933
Vice-President, Standard Paving & Materials Ltd.

Arnold C. Schmitz   1955–1963
Comptroller, Metal Fabricators & Roofing Ltd.

G. Richard Schulli   1951–1961
Supervisor, Ernst & Ernst, Chartered Accountants

Donald G. Scott   1931–1935, 1941–1947
*Vice-President, Administration & Finance,
Eldorado Mining and Refining Limited*

Douglas H. Scott   1954–1962
*Partner,
Lever, Hoskin, Chagnon & MacGillivray, Chartered Accountants*

G. Martyn Scott   1925–1937
Vice-President, Finance, Gordon Mackay and Company Limited

Norman L. Scott   1953–1959
Comptroller, Wilson Oilfield Supply Ltd.

V. W. T. Scully   1925–1933
President, The Steel Company of Canada Limited

V. Brad Secker   1946–1949
Secretary, The Boiler Inspection and Insurance Company of Canada

D. S. Sellars   1945–1949
Treasurer, R. M. Hollingshead Corporation of Canada Limited

Harold P. Sellers   1938–1940
*Partner,
Riddell, Stead, Graham & Hutchison, Chartered Accountants*

Roy E. Shannon   1958–1962
Vice-President, Inter-Lake Transport

David A. Shantz   1949–1957
Partner, Rogers & Rose, Chartered Accountants

G. D. Shearer   1956–1958
Controller, Hugh Russel & Sons Ltd.

C. Alec Shearson   1956–1962
Secretary, M.E.P.C. Canadian Properties Limited

T. G. Sheeres 1953–1961
Treasurer, Canadian Industrial Gas Limited

C. K. Shellard 1949–1954
Assessor, Taxation Division, Department of National Revenue

W. G. Shenson 1921–1925
Assessor, Income Tax Division, Department of National Revenue

H. Arnold Sherman 1956–1958
General Tax Manager, Massey-Ferguson Limited

A. Lawson Sherring 1930–1962
Trust Officer, National Trust Company Limited

John H. Shields 1957–1961
Manager, Kellys on Seymour Ltd.

R. M. Shields 1950–1952
Supervisor, Corporate Accounting, Imperial Oil Limited

E. A. Shillington 1954–1960
—

Carl A. Shore 1950–1955
Secretary-Treasurer, Port Weller Dry Docks Limited

J. S. Sidle 1958–1963
Comptroller, General Printers Limited

John H. Silverthorn 1943–1951
Regional Cost Accountant,
Hydro-Electric Power Commission of Ontario

Gordon E. Sims 1941–1944
Comptroller,
St. Clair Grain & Feeds, Division of Maple Leaf Mills Ltd.

J. A. Sinclair 1949–1956
Chief Accountant, White Pass & Yukon Route

S. J. Sinclair 1945–1948
President, Western Tire and Auto Supply Limited

W. M. Sinclair 1919–1925
In practice, Wilfred M. Sinclair, Chartered Accountant

William T. Sinclair 1949–1956
Canadian Manager, Daryl Products Corp. (Canada) Ltd.

Hugh G. Singleton 1928–1936
Secretary, Patons & Baldwins (Canada) Limited

R. E. Singleton 1941–1950
Controller, Canadian Pittsburgh Industries Ltd.

H. H. Sivers 1938–1946
Secretary-Treasurer, Bausch & Lomb Optical Co. Ltd.

G. R. W. Skerrett 1959–1963
Comptroller, The Elias Rogers Company Limited

Lawrence Wilton Skey 1934–1936
Director & Treasurer, Scudder International Investments Ltd.

G. Smallshaw 1949–1954
*Director of Mineral Audits,
Saskatchewan Department of Mineral Resources*

B. T. Smith 1956–1961
Internal Auditor, Consolidated Building Corporation Limited

Fred D. Smith 1945–1950
Comptroller and Treasurer, White Pass & Yukon Route

Hedley M. Smith 1928–1946
Comptroller, E. C. King Contracting Ltd.

H. Russell H. Smith 1930–1940, 1962–1963
Regional Audit Supervisor, Ontario Retail Sales Tax

K. L. Smith 1942–1952
Comptroller, Salada Foods Ltd.

Maxwell C. Smith 1950–1954
In practice, Maxwell C. Smith, Chartered Accountant

Rodney J. Smith 1949–1954
*Partner,
Gray, Butcher, Frost & Smith, Chartered Accountants*

W. Keith Smith 1955–1959
Consultant, Booz, Allen & Hamilton, Inc., Management Consultants

W. Angus Smyth 1935–1951
President, Rose & Laflamme Limited

William M. Smyth 1951–1955
Director of Purchasing & Packaging, John Labatt Limited

J. Douglas Snedden   1948–1952
Assistant Director and Controller,
The Hospital for Sick Children

D. M. Snell   1946–1953
Partner, Eddis & Associates, Chartered Accountants

R. J. Snell   1949–1950
In practice, R. J. Snell, Chartered Accountant

Victor J. Sobczuk   1962–1963
Chief Accountant, Economical Mutual Insurance Co.

W. Alec Spear   1918–1928
Retired

George H. Spence   1931–1938
Provincial Auditor, Province of Ontario

M. A. Spowart   1954–1957
Partner, Chadwick, Potts & Co., Chartered Accountants

G. H. Sprague   1933–1945
Treasurer, Atomic Energy of Canada Ltd.

D. C. Spratt   1952–1957
Lecturer (Accounting), Ryerson Polytechnical Institute

Jack Springstead   1958–1964
Manager of Corporate Trust Department,
The Royal Trust Company, Hamilton Branch

G. Douglas Spry   1946–1949
Comptroller of Finance,
Board of Education for the City of Toronto

Nowell A. Stables   1953–1956
Tax and Insurance Supervisor, Marathon Oil Company

Edward Stamp   1952–1962
Senior Lecturer, University of Wellington

Kenneth A. Stephen   1951–1954
Secretary-Treasurer, A. E. LePage Limited

F. I. Stephens   1945–1951
Squadron Leader, RCAF, Department of National Defence

H. Malcolm Stephens 1934–1940
Comptroller, Dominion Ayers Limited

C. H. G. Stevens 1950–1953
Comptroller, Canadian Pacific Oil and Gas Limited

Graham H. Stevens 1920–1925
Secretary-Treasurer, Z. Wagman & Son Limited

Lloyd F. Stevens 1942–1962
Executive Vice-President, Allpak Products Limited

F. J. E. Stewart 1955–1961

Wm. G. Stewart 1951–1955
Treasurer, Union Gas Company of Canada, Limited

D. H. Stodart 1937–1948
Vice-President, Canadian Trans Lux Corp. Ltd.

W. J. Stokes 1954–1959
Internal Auditor, St. Mary's Cement Co. Limited

Frank R. Stone 1932–1941
Vice-President (Administration), University of Toronto

Gerald M. Stone 1950–1957
Manager, London Office,
Campbell, Lawless & Punchard, Chartered Accountants

G. Stork 1959–1962
Assistant Comptroller, Zenith Electric Supply Limited

Harry F. Strathy 1930–1937
Accounting Department, McLeod, Young, Weir & Co. Ltd.

R. F. Strong 1952–1960
Assistant Manager, Caproco Corrosion Prevention Ltd.

L. D. Stupart 1917–1922
Retired

R. J. Sunberg 1957–1963
In practice, R. J. Sunberg, Chartered Accountant

R. R. Sutherland 1940–1956
Comptroller, Brazilian Traction, Light and Power Company, Limited

David G. Sweet 1955–1960
Partner, Russell & Du Moulin, Barristers & Solicitors

George E. Syme   1952–1956
Commercial Director, Silverthorn Collegiate Institute

Michael R. Tague   1958–1962
Teacher, Port Credit Secondary School

Walter D. Tamblyn   1934–1946
President, Tamblyn-Pritchard Construction Limited

W. C. Tate   1949–1955
Vice-President and General Manager, Garrett Manufacturing Ltd.

James C. Taylor   1938–1945
Professor,
School of Business Administration, University of Western Ontario

W. L. Taylor   1944–1950
Secretary-Treasurer, Toronto General Burying Grounds

L. C. Teskey   1923–1936
Partner, Teskey, Petrie & Burnside, Chartered Accountants

Arthur J. Thomas   1949–1957
Director & Comptroller, Deacon, Findley Coyne Limited

James D. Thomas   1948–1951
Vice-President/Director, West Coast Securities Ltd.

R. D. Thomas   1946–1950
Executive Secretary and Director of Research,
Canadian Institute of Chartered Accountants

J. D. Thompson   1953–1961
Comptroller, National System of Baking Ltd.

James C. Thompson   1936–1941
Partner, Peat, Marwick, Mitchell & Co., Chartered Accountants

John M. Thompson   1927–1939
Vice-President, Domtar Pulp & Paper Limited

V. J. Thompson   1945–1956
Comptroller, Smith Transport Limited

D. J. Thomson   1945–1953
Assistant Secretary-Treasurer, Pre-Con Murray Limited

E. B. Thomson   1944–1952
Comptroller, A. E. Ames & Co. Limited

John W. Thomson   1949–1956
President, Thomson Drilling Ltd.

Kathleen Thorne   1935–1946
Retired

Ronald C. Thornton   1951–1957
Chief Accountant, Don Mills Developments Ltd.

R. W. Ticknor   1945–1951
President, Queensway Volkswagen Co. Ltd.

W. D. Tidball   1952–1964
Chief Accountant, Calgary Exhibition & Stampede Limited

C. Frank Topp   1938–1943
*Superintendent of Operations & Services,
Henry Morgan & Co. Ltd.*

Frank A. Topping   1952–1956
Comptroller, Bristol Laboratories of Canada Ltd.

Ken Torrance   1955–1962
Toronto Office Accountant, Guaranty Trust Company of Canada

R. L. Towler   1953–1957
*In practice with
Barrow, Nicoll & Co., Chartered Accountants*

E. J. Trerise   1951–1952
In practice with H. R. Horne, Chartered Accountant

G. R. F. Troop   1924–1933
Retired

W. K. Trusler   1950–1951
In practice, Wm. K. Trusler, Chartered Accountant

Robert Turgeon   1954–1957
En pratique, R. Turgeon, Comptable Agréé

D. W. Turnbull   1938–1948
Vice-President & General Manager, Foster Advertising Ltd.

J. M. Turnbull   1936–1949
Comptroller, The British American Oil Company Limited

Archie C. Turner   1948–1960
Controller, Rio Algom Mines Limited

J. H. Turner   1943–1946
Partner, McColl, Turner & Co., Chartered Accountants

Douglas W. Tyndall   1949–1959
Assistant to President, McNamara Corporation Limited

E. N. Vanstone   1926–1934
Vice-President and Treasurer, Moore Corporation, Limited

Frank S. Vanstone   1917–1933
Secretary-Treasurer, St. Mary's Cement Co., Limited

J. Van Netten   1949–1956
Manager,
Corporate Financial Planning, Rio Algom Mines Limited

Thomas Van Zuiden   1943–1952
Assistant Secretary and Assistant Treasurer,
Dominion Foundries and Steel Limited

Jean Verville   1957–1959
Comptable en chef, Hôpital Hôtel-Dieu d'Arthabaska

Roy Vetzal   1949–1962
Assistant Controller, Atlas Steels Company Limited

R. G. Violette   1960–1964
Operations Research, Polymer Corporation Limited

K. I. Wagner   1955–1961
Accountant, The Windsor Star

Derek N. Walker   1953–1955
Secretary-Treasurer, Canadian Export Gas & Oil Ltd.

Ernest A. Walker   1958–1962
Partner, A. F. MacLaren & Co., Chartered Accountants

Michael A. Wallis   1940–1945
Manager, Financial & Tax Division,
Comptroller's Department, Imperial Oil Limited

Edward A. Walters   1950–1953
Director, Municipal Auditing, Accounting & Inspections,
Department of Municipal Affairs, Province of Saskatchewan

William C. Wansbrough   1953–1963
Assistant Comptroller, Pigott Construction Co. Ltd.

Cyril Ward 1951–1955
Controller, Pure Spring (Canada) Limited

Robert B. Ward 1951–1956
Resident Auditor, General Motors Diesel Limited

W. H. Wardle 1949–1954
Controller, Warner-Lambert Canada Limited

Frederick C. Waring 1955–1963
Comptroller, Shaw Pipe Protection Limited

H. William C. Watson 1960–1961
Assessor, Department of National Revenue

Clifford B. Watt 1926–1930
General Manager, Canadian Government Printing Bureau

N. M. Watt 1942–1948
Treasurer, Consolidated Frybrook Industries Limited

Donald I. Webb 1946–1955
Vice-President, Merrill, Lynch, Pierce, Fenner & Smith Inc.

R. L. Webber 1943–1946
Assistant Treasurer, Toronto Stock Exchange

Edward W. Webster 1945–1950
Controller, Tip Top Tailors Limited

Thomas Weir 1914–1937
Retired

Harry O. Weldon 1955–1959
In practice, Harry O. Weldon, Chartered Accountant

Harold G. Wenaus 1959–1963
Supervisor, Provincial Audit Office, Province of Saskatchewan

R. A. West 1946–1955
President, National Leased Assets Limited

Bruno V. W. Westerlund 1956–1962
Controller, Hume & Rumble Limited

Elliott Whiteman 1959–1960
Business Assessor, Department of National Revenue

R. Kenneth Whitley 1952–1956, 1961–1963
Corporate Controller, Crane Canada Limited

J. Gordon Wicijowski 1955–1959
In practice, J. Gordon Wicijowski, Chartered Accountant

E. M. B. Wickham 1953–1956
Assessor, Department of National Revenue

Duane E. Wikant 1953–1959
Secretary-Treasurer, Canadian Homestead Oils Limited

G. Ray Wildblood 1940–1948
Business Administrator, Oshawa Clinic

M. Elizabeth Williams 1943–1953
Secretary-Treasurer, F. H. Hayhurst Co. Limited

Peter H. Williams 1949–1952
Revenue Department, Government of Ontario

Roy G. Williams 1959–1960
Partner, Thacker & Williams, Chartered Accountants

Bruce C. Willis 1936–1949
Partner, P. S. Ross & Partners, Management Consultants

J. R. Willson 1952–1959
Assistant Controller, Mueller, Limited

A. C. Wilson 1938–1941
Assistant Secretary-Treasurer, Schwabacher-Frey Company

D. Fraser Wilson 1924–1929
*Executive Assistant to the Vice-President, Finance,
The T. Eaton Co. Ltd.*

F. N. Wilson 1940–1950
*Vice-President & Treasurer,
Canada & Dominion Sugar Company Ltd.*

George C. Wilson 1955–1959
Planning Assistant, Imperial Life Assurance Co. of Canada

J. E. Wilson 1932–1941
McCarthy & McCarthy, Barristers & Solicitors

J. F. Wilson 1952–1957
Internal Auditor, Pacific Petroleums Ltd.

James C. Wilson 1932–1938
*Partner,
Peat, Marwick, Mitchell & Co., Chartered Accountants*

Roy B. Wilson   1955–1960
Controller, Varian Associates of Canada Ltd.

C. H. Windeler   1921–1929
Secretary, Noranda Mines, Limited

Gordon T. Wishart   1930–1940
Vice-President and General Manager, Metals & Alloys Co. Ltd.

Bertrand Wolfman   1960–1962
Consultant, P. S. Ross & Partners, Management Consultants

A. S. Wolfson   1956–1958
Assistant to Comptroller, Allied Chemical Canada Ltd.

Frank W. Woods   1935–1946
Secretary, Moore Corporation, Limited

Kenneth S. Woods   1951–1953
Assistant Retail Administration, Simpson-Sears Limited

Ian C. Woolley   1946–1950
Assistant Secretary-Treasurer,
Dominion Securities Corporation Ltd.

R. G. Wright   1947–1958
Treasurer, Bayer Foreign Investments Limited

Donald F. Wyckoff   1944–1948
Controller, Parts and Accessories, Sales Division,
Ford Motor Company of Canada, Limited

T. E. Yates   1957–1962
Secretary-Treasurer,
British & American Chevrolet Oldsmobile Ltd.

Douglas A. Young   1962
Financial Analyst, Chrysler Corporation of Canada Ltd.

M. Arnold **Young**   1941–1950
Accountant, Geo. & L. H. Leaver

Adam H. Zimmerman   1950–1958
Comptroller, Noranda Mines, Limited

APPENDIX III

FORMER PERSONNEL OF
WOODS GORDON & CO.,
AND THEIR POSITIONS AT JULY 1, 1964*

Wm. T. Andrews 1946–1950
Project Officer, Missile Systems,
Department of Defence Production

Aubrey W. Baillie 1931–1934
President, Bowes Company Ltd.

John J. Carson 1946–1952
Manager, Staff Services Division,
British Columbia Hydro and Power Authority

John A. Carter 1952–1956
Manager, Data Processing Department,
The T. Eaton Co. Ltd.

R. F. Chisholm 1934–1938
Executive Vice-President, Dominion Stores Limited

V. S. B. Corbet 1946–1953
General Production Manager, Consumers Glass Company Limited

L. M. Cuddy 1951–1953
Director of Manufacturing, Allied Chemical Canada Ltd.

*This does not include those who are also listed as former personnel
of Clarkson, Gordon & Co. and the Clarkson Company Limited

H. M. S. Ferguson   1937–1947
Manager, Standards Department,
Dominion Textile Company Limited

John G. Fleming   1956–1960
President, Pozlan Industries Ltd.

George Taylor Fulford III   1957–1958
President, Brockville Shopping Centre Ltd.

Matthew Gaasenbeek   1956–1959
Director in Charge of Underwriting,
Annett & Company Limited

T. C. Graham   1937–1950
Professor, School of Business, University of Toronto

H. C. Grant   1945–1949
Associate Director, Management Advisory Services,
Deloitte, Plender, Haskins & Sells, Chartered Accountants

Roland A. Harris   1939–1940
Vice-President, Marketing, B. F. Goodrich Canada Limited

Norman W. Hayman   1959–1964
Director of Manufacturing, Dominion Forge Company

R. W. Henwood   1933–1938
President, Laurentian Spring Water Ltd.

James F. Hickling   1946–1947
President,
Canadian Personnel Consultants &
Hickling Executive Placement Ltd.

Rob't. W. Hipwell   1946–1951
Manager, Industrial Engineering,
Peat, Marwick, Mitchell & Co., Chartered Accountants

Robert S. Innes   1956–1958
General Manager, Canadian Bird Equipment Ltd.

A. J. Paul LaPrairie   1958–1960
Manager, Manufacturing Division, Procor Limited

J. M. Lougheed   1933–1937
Supervisor, Time Study Department,
Canadian Acme Screw & Gear Ltd. (Levy Industries)

Clifford Luxton 1952–1957
Executive Assistant to the General Manager,
Wallaceburg Brass Limited

Dr. J. W. Macmillan 1953
Director, Personnel-Development, Canada Packers Ltd.

Dr. E. D. MacPhee 1933–1940
Dean Emeritus,
University of British Columbia;
Dean, Banff School of Advanced Management

R. K. Martin 1942–1943
President, Martin, Lucas & Co. Ltd.

D. C. Matthews 1950–1953
President, Schooner Corporation Limited

Paul D. Matthews 1953–1957
Assistant to the Manager, Plastic Films,
Union Carbide Canada Ltd.

George M. McGregor 1944–1960
Vice-President & General Manager,
Donald Ropes & Wire Cloth Limited

J. A. McIntyre 1951–1952
Director, Department of Extension
University of Western Ontario

James A. McLachlin 1948–1951
Manager, Industrial & Plant Engineering,
Office Specialty Ltd.

John M. Milne 1952–1953
President, Pemberton, Freeman, Mathes & Milne

J. N. Moxon 1950–1953
Partner, Hutchins, Mullin & Blair, Chartered Accountants

Arthur R. Neufeld 1947–1956
President & General Manager,
Caneng Manufacturing Company Ltd.

Philip N. O'Hara 1956–1963
Director of Computer and Communications,
Toronto Stock Exchange

R. J. Orr 1959
Director of Marketing, Studebaker of Canada, Limited

John D. Pawling 1948–1953
General Manager, Carton Specialties Division,
Domtar Packaging Ltd.

R. A. Read 1946–1957
Vice-President & General Manager,
R. Laidlaw Lumber Co. Ltd.

W. J. Rice 1960–1963
Manager, Methods Control Department,
Dominion of Canada General Insurance Co.

B. H. Rieger 1941–1950
Vice-President, Canadian Corporate Management Co. Ltd.

John L. S. Ross 1945–1950
Plant Superintendent, John Wood Co. Ltd.

George W. Rutledge 1952–1963
Investment Officer, Power Corporation of Canada Limited

John C. Sawatsky 1948–1949
Associate Professor, School of Business, University of Toronto

Robert C. A. Waddell 1947–1959
Cochran, Murray & Company Limited

Philip E. Wheatley 1957–1960
Comptroller, British Rubber Co. Ltd.

R. L. Wright 1947–1953
General Manager, Muntz & Beatty Ltd.

Herbert Young 1953–1956
Vice-President & General Manager, Dominion Forge Co.

APPENDIX IV

PERSONNEL OF CLARKSON GORDON & CO.
AND THE CLARKSON COMPANY LIMITED
AT JULY 1, 1964

QUEBEC

PARTNER—ASSOCIÉ

Raymond Normandeau

MANAGERS—GÉRANTS

Jean Carrier, Guy Gingras

PROFESSIONAL STAFF—PERSONNEL PROFESSIONNEL

Michel Bernier, Pierre Bidégaré, Guy Breton,
Gamelin Lavoie, Clément Létourneau

ADMINISTRATIVE STAFF—PERSONNEL ADMINISTRATIF

Lyne Carmichael

MONTREAL

PARTNERS—ASSOCIÉS

R. Victor Barnett, Harry Elliot Bell, Marcel Camirand,
H. Marcel Caron, Jérôme Carrière, Donald J. Finley,
John B. Gick, Arthur W. Gilmour, George P. Keeping,
Kenneth A. MacKenzie, John D. Morrison, Donald C. Scott

Marguerite Roy, Patricia Tickell, Sandra Tuckwell,
Aline L. Vincent

TORONTO

PARTNERS

Col. H. D. Lockhart Gordon

Thomas P. Abel, G. A. Adamson, Rodney J. Anderson,
John L. Biddell, G. K. Carr, G. P. Clarkson,
G. E. Cronkwright, H. C. Dell, John W. Dickson,
R. W. E. Dilworth, W. A. Farlinger, J. Eric Ford,
E. A. C. Freeman-Attwood, Kerr Gibson, Duncan L. Gordon,
Eric H. Johnston, David W. Lay, A. J. Little,
W. L. MacDonald, Michael Mackenzie,
R. MacDonald Parkinson, G. G. Richardson, W. Grant Ross,
Ross M. Skinner, A. H. Wait, J. R. M. Wilson,
David H. Wishart, Michael E. Wright

MANAGERS

E. J. Barringham, E. O. Bentley, James Bunton,
Robert W. Cameron, Elmer A. Campbell, Kerr M. Chalmers,
Geoffrey W. Clarkson, J. Murray Cockburn,
George S. Dembroski, John A. Dossett, E. Austin Fricker,
G. Taylor Gilbert, H. F. Colin Graham, John G. Greene,
David M. Hector, Brian R. Hockey, Donald C. Hoover,
Murray G. Kingsburgh, John Kirkwood, P. J. Lewis,
David G. R. Lindsay, Gilbert A. Little, W. H. Lynn,
Frederick S. Mallett, Alexander D. McIntosh, William R. Miller,
P. C. Monachan, Donald S. Muir, Ian S. Murdoch,
Barry D. Nicol, Irving Nyman, Wayne Penny, R. S. Pepler,
Martin Reaume, Laurence H. Ritchie, Gordon T. Robertson,
Allen D. Russell, Barry M. Smith, Ronald E. Strange,
Robert R. Topp, F. J. Troop, William E. Wait,
W. J. Walker, Calvin K. Wenaus, J. J. Wigle,
N. H. Witherell, David A. Yule

PROFESSIONAL STAFF

N. Abramsen, Keith Acheson, Eric R. Adams,
Peter Mitchell Adamson, Clifford W. Addison,
Malcolm G. L. Aikman, John Alderson, Peter K. E. Allan,
K. A. Alles, Allan G. Andrews, John Murray Armitage,

Peter J. Armstrong, R. Paul Arnold, John H. Atcheson,
C. T. Austin, Edwin W. Austin, William F. Avery,
Robert F. Baker, William H. Banfield, Peter Barker,
Roy Barnett, Lawrence S. Barrett, Ian D. Bayer,
Peter T. Bogart, R. E. Boone, Edgar A. Bracht,
David Ian Butler, John J. Calnan, James W. Carter,
W. Brian Carter, E. Barry Christian, B. Neil Clark,
Donald Fergus Clark, W. James Clark, C. E. Conaghan,
Horace A. Corrigan, Graham Cosserat, Alex J. Cox,
Douglas A. Cox, John A. Craven, William Ewart Crawford,
R. Allan Curran, Donald J. Dal Bianco, Robert M. Davies,
M. Barry Dent, Paul J. de Winter, W. Grant Dickenson,
Albert J. J. Dockrell, Michael L. Doody, Joan Douglas,
P. B. Dunlop, Ronald G. Dunne, Otto J. Eaton,
Douglas N. Farr, Peter M. Farwell, Gordon A. Fear,
Robert Fenn, David E. Friesen, R. E. Fuller, Ronald G. Gage,
Donald Gard, Robert E. Garland, Robert J. Gatfield,
Ronald Gilbart, James E. Gillies, Robert E. Giroux,
Dimitar Golubov, Anthony Gooch, Crawford Gordon,
Glenn W. Gordon, J. Malcolm Gourlay, J. Douglas Grant,
John H. Gray, Robert Hall, Peter V. Hamley, G. Ross Harding,
Morgan Thomas Harris, Owen H. Hay, Nicholas Heffer,
Paul J. Heffernan, David H. Hills, John G. Hood,
Robert W. Howard, Andrew B. Hughes, David G. Hurlburt,
Pierre J. Hurschler, Allan S. Inglis, K. L. Ingo,
Philip John Jenkinson, Z. P. Jerabek, Patrick Albert Jordan,
Craig L. Judson, Gopal Karna, Alan Kemp-Gee,
Richard W. Kempe, Peter G. LaFlair, Norman W. Laine,
A. R. W. Large, Charles A. Latimer, L. Philippe Leclair,
Sidney A. Lindsay, John Liphardt, Robert G. Long,
Robert E. Lord, S. Michael Loskow, Stephens B. Lowden,
R. Howard MacDonald, Donald MacIntyre, Donald A. MacIver,
Donald A. MacNeill, Stephen W. March, R. Fraser Mason,
Donald A. Matheson, Roderick A. McCulloch,
Edward M. McGovern, G. L. Meadows, John Meek,
Robert J. Meldrum, Alan Mellor, Peter M. H. Menzies,
R. E. Metcalfe, Robert A. Michaud, J. Alexander Milburn,
Richard D. Miles, M. D. Minshull, Robert A. Mitchell,
T. E. Monteith, Blair L. Morley, Noel C. Morton,

Koji Nakai, G. N. Nichols, William R. Nolan,
Kenneth J. Ogle, David J. Ogus, Norman R. Oldfield,
Renzo Orlando, Theodore Orlans, Edmund G. Osler,
John A. Palmer, H. Richard C. Pedlar, William L. Porter,
Robert C. Price, Michael C. Proctor, John F. Rahn,
Otto E. Renelt, David I. Richardson, John F. Ricketts,
J. Nicholas Ross, Michael C. Ross, Michael Samuel,
Louis A. Sattler, Robert Savage, Terence P. Scandrett,
Samuel M. Schaffran, Donald Scott, Peter D. Scott,
Ronald W. Scott, David Selley, David E. Sharpe,
J. Keith Shepherd, C. Peter Shirriff, David M. Smith,
P. W. Smith, William J. Smith, Gordon Spence,
George D. Stephens, Robert B. Stevenson, Robert John Stirling,
Howard J. Stollery, Robert R. Stone, Ian K. Strang,
John M. Swinden, James R. Symington,
D. M. H. B. Tamitegama, Barry Tannock, David Tate,
Bruce W. Taylor, Douglas A. Taylor, O. B. Thibaudeau,
Alan R. Thomas, Terence T. Thompson, Peter I. Vallis,
Robert Bruce Wallace, James M. Ward, James A. Wareing,
William B. Waterbury, Victor A. Wells,
Robert A. Wilkinson, C. J. Woodward, D. S. Wright,
James A. Wylie, S. J. Zysman

ADMINISTRATIVE STAFF

Donald K. Durst, *Comptroller*
R. L. King, *Secretary-Treasurer*
K. H. C. Laundy, *Director of Education*
John D. Stohn, *Director of Personnel*
Diane E. Allcock, Gwendolyn M. Anderson,
Josephine M. Arney, Doris A. Bateman, N. Bates,
Eileen M. Beckett, Audrey L. Benson, Rosemarie Bergen,
D. Ruth Bonner, Grace S. Bonner, Gloria H. Boone,
Veronika Both, Carole M. Burgess, Mary E. Cantwell,
Alberta Carr, Olive M. Chin, Glenna G. Christie, Ruth E. Coe,
Ilga A. Colberg, Susan M. Cooper, Myrtle M. Cumming,
Janet Cunningham, Audrey E. Dance, Ernestine Dowe,
Marion E. Duncan, Sylvia Ego, Blair Enman,
Josephine H. Fagan, Beverley J. Fawcett, Elva L. Ferris,
Marice C. Fitzpatrick, Jean Frankum, Gail Gervais,

Gloria D. Glas, Anne Grinevicius, Claire Haley,
Deborah Harakas, Shirley Hassler, Karen Hazell,
Betty Hendry, Jean E. Henry, Ursula Hirschfeld,
Joan T. Hollaran, Catherine P. Hyde, Dorothy L. Jackson,
Joan Johnson, Paul Jones, Anneliese Jurock,
Darwina L. Keywan, Elaine LaLiberte, Ruth P. Lambert,
F. E. Leitch, Carol Lessard, Eleanor Lilley, Ann J. Lindahl,
Judith A. Mackness, Susan D. Matthews, Kathleen T. McAleese,
Ruth E. McClellan, Cynthia McDonald, Helen M. McHale,
Margaret McIntosh, Mary M. McLaughlin,
Isabel M. Minoughan, Gwendolyne Morgan,
Doreen W. Morris, Nancy Nicol,
Margaret J. Osachuk, Patricia Parker, Alice R. Pollard,
Eleanor R. Porte, Patricia Powell, Dawn Quinn,
Evelyn I. Rennie, Mildred A. Riddell, Eileen M. Rogers,
Elsie Rue, Carol A. Shields, Ingrid Schultz, Ruby A. Smith,
Pamela M. Stevens, Amaryllis G. Stewart, Dorothy G. Sumner,
Elizabeth M. Szeli, Barabara J. Terris, Shirley C. Terris,
L. Jean Thomson, Eileen N. Unroth, Norma W. Van Horne,
Patricia A. Waring, John M. Willems, Gwendoline Williams,
Helen Wilson, Charles H. Winney, Marilyn Wise,
Raymond C. Yawching, Marguerite Zielinski

HAMILTON

PARTNERS

E. H. Ambrose, Harold C. Dixon, Walter J. Smith

MANAGERS

Murray T. Collier, Paul A. Southall, Brooke P. Townsend,
William G. Wilson

PROFESSIONAL STAFF

Jack Brown, J. Clifford Collingwood, J. Edward T. Dillane,
John A. Gabriel, Murray R. Halpren, George S. Hamilton,
R. Keith McAlpine, R. Douglas McCaw, David W. Moyer,
Morton Nelson, G. Wayne Perry, Barbara Pindar,
Rein Reio, Daniel B. Robinson, Harold H. Serabian,
Owen C. Shewfelt, William A. Sims

Edward E. Manser, Carl F. Nelles, William K. Powers,
Frederick Ritzmann, Richard E. Shuel, Tommy J. Siemash

Betty Lou Dell, Vernonica Valuck

WINNIPEG

Stanley J. Haughey, Allan M. Moore, William E. Shields

Donald L. Lucyk, Henry J. Pankratz, Gilbert A. Wilde

Leon A. Ballegeer, D. Gordon Bentham, Robert C. A. Brown,
Allan F. Budlong, Murray J. Halliday, Isadore M. Hnybida,
Lawrence M. Hurtig, Harold W. Kupchak, John D. Kuryluk,
Robert J. A. Lord, Arthur E. Magner, P. Dale Magnus,
Bryan J. McCammon, John A. McDermid, Ralph K. Palmer,
David Petrie, Dennis D. Robinson, Ronald M. T. Topping,
William M. Willson

Betty A. Baird, Geraldine O. Clarkin, Mary A. Giles,
Helen E. Seabury

REGINA

W. E. Clarke, Ian Forbes

W. H. Edwards, P. A. Gebert

B. C. Davies, R. G. Downie, W. Rand Flynn,
G. E. Franklin, G. T. Gourlay, A. L. Pomeroy,
R. G. Howorth, R. A. Leitner, Leonard J. Serdachny,
R. F. T. Willows, R. R. Windrem

M. Lillian McDonald, Linda J. McLean

EDMONTON

CALGARY

APPENDIX V

PERSONNEL OF WOODS, GORDON & CO. AT JULY 1, 1964

MONTREAL

PARTNERS—ASSOCIÉS

H. Marcel Caron, R. Davidson, H. W. Rowlands,
G. G. Tremblay, D. M. Turnbull

SENIOR CONSULTANT—CONSEILLER-SENIOR

Claude Lemieux

CONSULTANTS—CONSEILLERS

P. E. Bieler, J. F. Clairoux, G. A. D'Amour, G. A. Gagnon,
G. R. Williams

ASSOCIATE—CONSEIL

J. E. Dion

TORONTO

PARTNERS

G. B. Bailey, James A. Brown, E. B. Chown,
G. P. Clarkson, Duncan L. Gordon, R. H. Grant,
Harold B. Guilfoyle, A. J. Little, J. A. Lowden,
Donald G. McLaren, R. O. Moore, Peter E. Newdick,
R. J. Shirley, J. M. Smith, Alan N. Steiner, David B. Watson

ACCOUNTING HISTORY AND THOUGHT

An Empirical Study of Financial Disclosure by Swedish Companies.
T. E. Cooke

Accountability of Local Authorities in England and Wales, 1831–1935.
Edited by Malcolm Coombs and J. R. Edwards

Accounting Methodology and the Work of R. J. Chambers
Michael Gaffikin

Schmalenbach's *Dynamic Accounting* and Price-Level Adjustments.
An Economic Consequences Explanation
O. Finley Graves, Graeme Dean, and Frank Clarke

An Analysis of the Early Record Keeping in the Du Pont Company, 1800–1818.
Roxanne Therese Johnson

The Closure of the Accounting Profession
Edited by T. A. Lee

Shareholder Use and Understanding of Financial Information
T. A. Lee and D. P. Tweedie

The Selected Writings of Maurice Moonitz
Maurice Moonitz

Methodology and Method in History
A Bibliography
Edited by Lee D. Parker and O. Finley Graves

Accounting in Australia
Historical Essays
Edited by Robert H. Parker

*The Growth of Arthur Andersen & Co., 1928–1973
Leonard Spacek

The Cash Recovery Rate Approach to the Estimation of Economic Performance
Edited by Andrew W. Stark

*Studies in Accounting Theory
Edited by W. T. Baxter

The Story of the Firm, 1864–1964,
Clarkson Gordon & Co.

A Half-Century of Accounting, 1899–1949
The Story of F. W. Lafrentz & Co.

Touche Ross
A Biography
Theodore Swanson

The District Auditor
Leonard Mervyn Helmore

*Academy of Accounting Historians Classics Series

Garland publishes books on all aspects of the accounting profession; for a complete list of titles please contact the publisher.